20 Bicycle Tours in the Five Boroughs

A Cyclist's Guide to New York City

Sandy Wolferman

Photographs by the author

A 20 Bicycle Tours™ Guide

Backcountry Publications
The Countryman Press, Inc.
Woodstock, Vermont

An Invitation to the Reader

Although it is unlikely that the roads you cycle on these tours will change much with time, some road signs, landmarks, and other items may. If you find that changes have occurred on these routes, please let us know so that we may correct them in future editions. The author and publisher also welcome other comments and suggestions. Address all correspondence:

Editor
20 Bicycle Tours™ Series
Backcountry Publications, Inc.
P.O. Box 175
Woodstock, Vermont 05091

Library of Congress Cataloging-in-Publication Data

Wolferman, Sandy, 1949–
20 bicycle tours in the five boroughs.
(A 20 bicycle tours guide)
1. Cycling—New York (N.Y.)—Guide-books. 2. New York (N.Y.)—Description—1981- —Guide-books.
I. Title: Twenty bicycle tours in the five boroughs.
II. Title.
GV1045.5.N72N498 1989 917.47'1 89-14997
ISBN 0-88150-143-3

Published by Backcountry Publications
A division of the Countryman Press, Inc.
Woodstock, Vermont 05091

Printed in the United States of America
Typesetting by Sant Bani Press
Text and cover design by Richard Widhu
Maps by Richard Widhu, © 1989 Backcountry Publications
Cover photograph is the view from Roosevelt Island

Publisher's notice: Cycling involves inherent risks, and readers planning to follow tours in this book should first read carefully the "safety" section of the introduction. Cyclists in urban areas should also be alert to the problem of crime. Tours in this book are in areas considered safe to ride in at the time of publication, but cyclists should follow sensible precautions (such as never cycling at night and traveling with one or more companions) and should be alert to changing patterns of crime in the city.

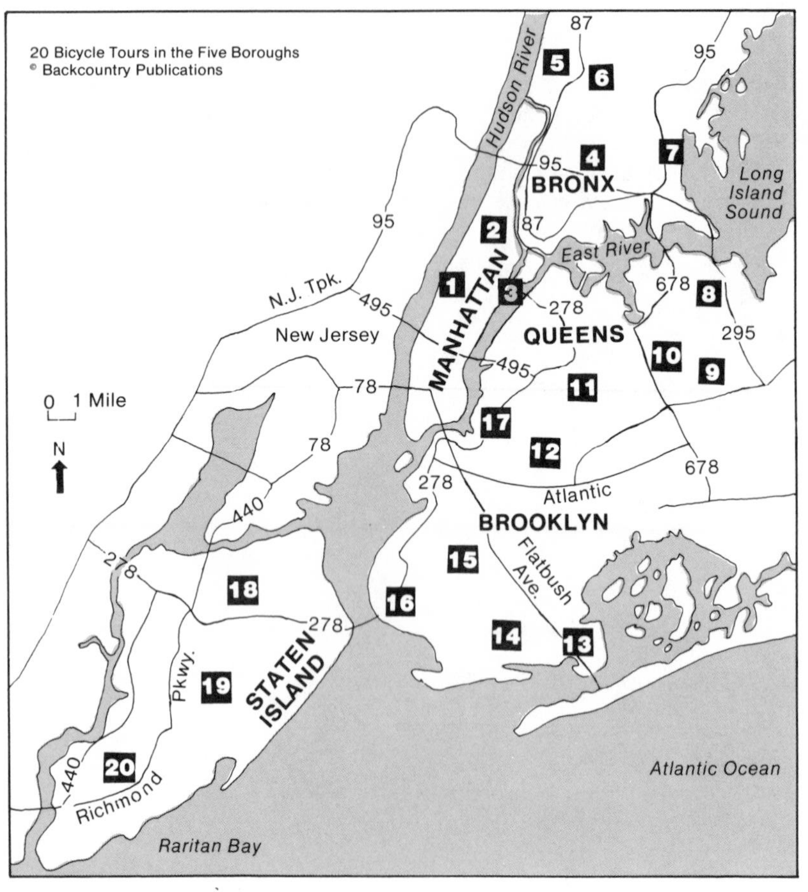
20 Bicycle Tours in the Five Boroughs
© Backcountry Publications
Hudson River
Long Island Sound
BRONX
East River
MANHATTAN
QUEENS
New Jersey
N.J. Tpk.
0 1 Mile
N
Atlantic
BROOKLYN
Flatbush Ave.
STATEN ISLAND
Pkwy.
Richmond
Raritan Bay
Atlantic Ocean
87
95
495
278
678
295
78
440
1
2
3
4
5
6
7
8
9
10
11
12
13
14
15
16
17
18
19
20

Contents

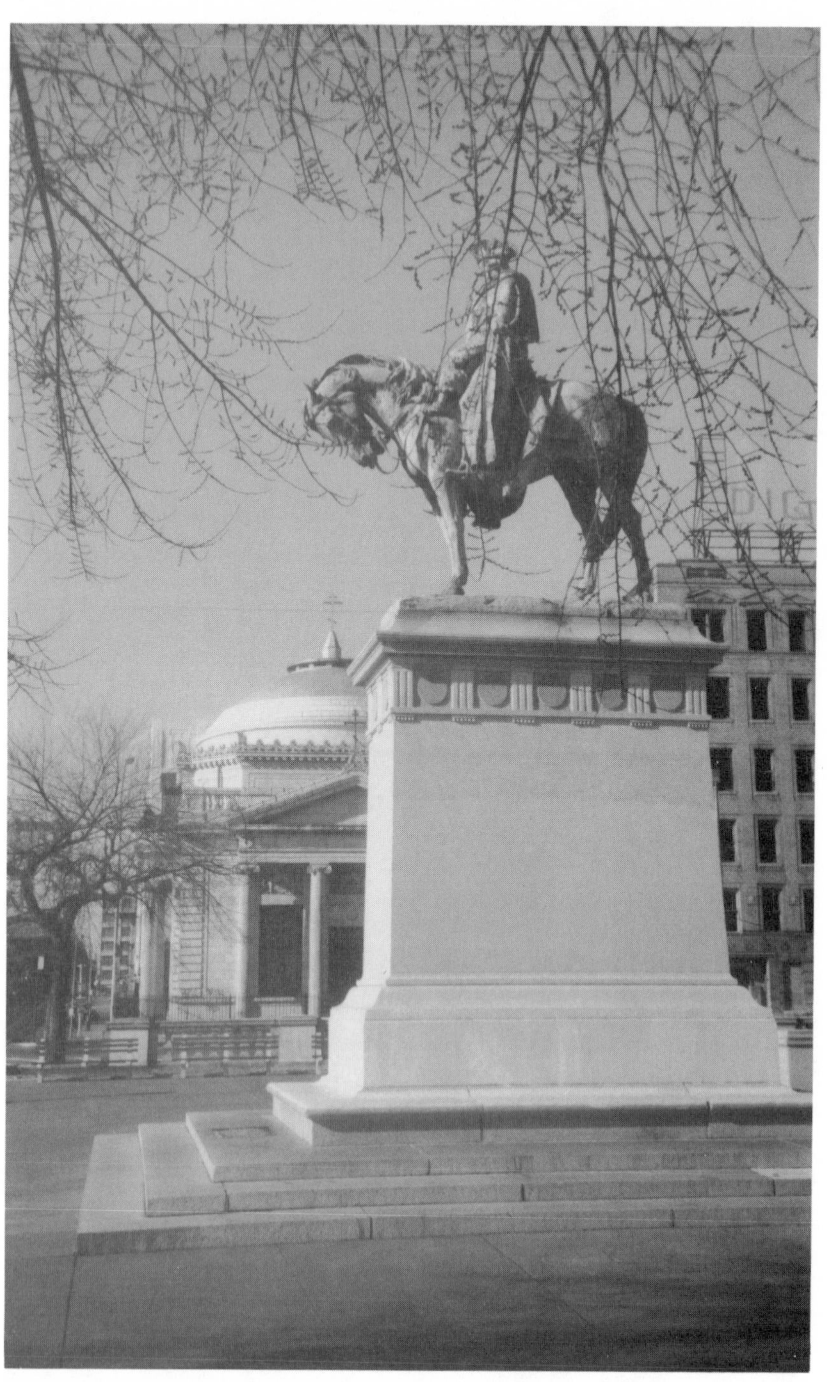

Washington Plaza in Williamsburg.

Introduction

Every day thousands of bicyclists battle pedestrians, pushcarts, and potholes for a share of New York City's congested thoroughfares. Yet there are also *hundreds of miles* of traffic-free bikeways and lightly traveled roads *within the five boroughs of New York City* where cyclists can pedal at a comfortable pace past a phenomenal array of communities and attractions. Ethnic neighborhoods, historic districts, architectural landmarks, museums, parks, zoos, beaches, bays, bridges, and bird sanctuaries await the cyclist who knows both where to find them and how to get around the city on two wheels with a minimum of hassle. New York City bicyclists needn't travel long distances by car, with bicycle in tow, to enjoy a few hours' or a day's pedaling away from the congestion and cacophony of the city's busiest roadways. The twenty rides presented here are all located within the city limits and are distributed throughout the five boroughs so that every resident can find a tour that begins near his or her doorstep.

About the Tours

The rides range in length from eleven to twenty-four miles. While most of the circular routes can be completed in less that two to two and a half hours of uninterrupted pedaling, they can just as easily be drawn out to half-day, or even full-day, affairs with visits to museums, parks, beaches, and other attractions listed along each route. In addition to giving the total and cumulative mileages, each ride features information on terrain and traffic conditions; a general description of the tour area and its points of interest; turn-by-turn directions; and a detailed map.

As a coastal city, New York is essentially flat, yet with enough minor variations in *terrain* to make bicycle-riding fun and interesting without being tiring. The tours are rated "flat," "rolling," or "hilly" according to the degree of topographical challenge. Generally speaking, Brooklyn is the flattest borough, with very little variation; Manhattan and Queens are rolling, with plenty of ups and downs of a gentle nature; and parts of Staten Island and the Bronx are hilly enough that some of us must push our bikes up the steeper inclines.

Traffic, of course, is the urban cyclist's nightmare. These routes have been plotted very carefully to avoid major traffic arteries and to make maximum use of traffic-free bikeways and lightly traveled roads throughout the five boroughs. Traffic is rated "light," "moderate," or "heavy." Unless otherwise stated, these ratings refer to weekend traffic conditions. Except in the remotest areas, traffic will always be somewhat heavier on business days. Avoiding traffic is a matter of common sense. Those who head for Coney Island on the Fourth of July, or cross the Queensborough Bridge at five P.M. on a Friday afternoon, will have plenty of company on the road. Conversely, those who tour lower Manhattan on a Sunday morning will enjoy wide-open streets, as will those who head for a seashore area in late fall.

Each tour is also preceded by a brief *description* of the area to be covered. Read these through carefully. In addition to providing a bit of historical background, they include information that is helpful in selecting a tour, in deciding what to bring and how much time to allow for the ride, and in preparing for any difficulties that may be encountered in a particular area (poor road conditions or a shortage of parking facilities, for example). The *points of interest* are described more fully as they present themselves along the route. These range from world-famous tourist attractions such as the Metropolitan Museum of Art and Times Square to obscure sites known only to local residents and historical societies, such as the Sleight family burial ground on Staten Island or the Quaker meeting house in Flushing. In between these two extremes is an assortment of sights and diversions wide enough to provide many hours of activity and sightseeing. The hours of access, admission fees, and availability of bike racks are included where applicable.

The *maps* in this book, together with the written *directions,* are sufficient to guide the cyclist through the tours. However, it is helpful to carry a borough map or pocket atlas as well. While the data in this volume were accurate at the time of publication, New York is a vibrant, growing city. A construction boom and a highway-improvement plan are changing the face of the city, especially in developing sections of the outer boroughs. Occasionally streets are eliminated or rerouted to make way for new construction; roads are torn up for the installation of new sewer or water pipes; and street names seem to change with alarming frequency. Should you encounter such an impasse, your borough map or atlas will come in handy in detouring around the blockage.

Safety for Urban Cyclists

City cycling needn't be any more hazardous than suburban and country cycling, as long as the cyclist observes a few guidelines.

1. Ride in the same direction as traffic. On two-way streets, this means staying as far to the right as possible. On the one-way avenues, it is best to stay left to avoid buses.

2. Use bicycle lanes when they are available. In the summer of 1980, Mayor Koch inaugurated a system of bicycle lanes on some of the major avenues in the city. These 4-foot-wide lanes are marked at intervals with white diamonds. Although you are certainly better off in a

bicycle lane than elsewhere on the road, do not assume that it is some sort of "safe zone" where you can relax your vigilance. Most motorists simply ignore the bike lanes, whether by intent or ignorance. Doors swing open into the lanes from parked cars; taxicabs pick up and discharge passengers there; and pedestrians and pushcarts lumber along them. Nevertheless, if you stay in the bike lane, you'll be on the right side of the law should any dispute arise.

3. Yield to pedestrians. In New York City, the majority of complaints against reckless bicyclists are filed not by motorists but by pedestrians. In a recent year over seven hundred bike-pedestrian collisions were reported to the police department. Do not assume that people see you. Be alert, scan ahead, and anticipate the pedestrian who suddenly steps off the curb to cross the street against a red light. In the event of a collision, he or she will get more sympathy than you will, no matter who had the right of way.

4. Wear a helmet. Using the right helmet can eliminate nearly all serious head injuries in bicycle accidents. The best models have a light-colored outer shell for visibility, an energy-absorbing liner of polystyrene or Styrofoam, strong straps and fasteners that will not release on impact, and adequate ventilation for comfort.

5. Observe traffic signals, including stop signs, traffic lights, and other warnings.

6. Equip your bicycle with an audible warning device such as a bell or a horn. Whistles are illegal in New York City.

7. Use hand signals when turning. Be particularly vigilant when making left turns. Some purists recommend that you stop, get off the bike, and walk across before making a left turn.

8. Ride single file only, keeping several bike-lengths between cyclists.

9. Wear light-colored clothing, and equip your bicycle with reflectors. Even if you do not plan to be out after dark, be prepared for the unexpected delay that might have you pedaling home after sundown. New York City streets are brightly lit at night; the problem is not seeing but being seen.

10. Before any ride, check your bicycle for mechanical defects. Loose bolts, sticky brakes, frayed cables, bald tires, and wobbly wheels are all potentially hazardous conditions and require attention before any trip.

Bike Security

Guarding against bicycle theft is a matter of common sense, as is investing in the best lock you can afford. While bicycle theft is a serious problem in urban areas, police department statistics indicate that bicycle thefts in New York City have actually been declining since the 1970s.

The Wycoff-Bennett house.

This is attributed to the use of U-shaped shackle locks (such as the Kryptonite® or Citadel®), which were introduced at that time. These locks offer much better security than chains or wire cables, which can be split with a bolt cutter or a hacksaw. In addition to investing in the best lock you can afford, observe the following precautions:

1. Lock your bike in a visible, well-trafficked public place.
2. Secure as much of the bike as possible to the rack or post. If you have quick-release hubs, remove the front wheel, then thread the chain or cable through the front wheel, frame, *and* the rear wheel. Some people carry two locking devices—one to attach the frame to the post, the other to attach the front wheel to the frame.
3. Remove all accessories (pump, light, water bottle) before leaving the bike.
4. Register the bicycle with the local police department. The police will record the serial number and stamp an identification number on the frame to help identify the bike if it is stolen and disguised.

Personal Safety

While bicycle theft is a nuisance we all hope to avoid, one's personal safety is a far more serious matter than loss of property. Fear of crime should not deter anybody from enjoying the city's parks and recreational opportunities, but bicyclists should be aware that attacks on cyclists, though rare, have occurred in deserted sections of city parks and on the streets late at night. Women alone are especially vulnerable and should avoid riding alone for the first time in areas of the city with which they are totally unfamiliar or in areas known to have higher than average crime rates. For maximum security, always stay on the designated route and, most of all, restrict your activities to daylight hours when crime is much less likely to take place.

Equipment

A major advantage of urban cycling is that you are never far from sources of food and water, bicycle-repair services, entertainment, or anything else you may require on a short ride. This greatly reduces the need to carry a lot of extraneous baggage. Still, for the sake of safety and convenience, it helps to carry a few basic items:

1. Tool kit. A six-inch adjustable wrench, a couple of Allen wrenches, a small Phillips-head screwdriver, a small pair of pliers, tire irons, and a patch kit will handle most minor roadside repairs.
2. Pump.
3. Lock and chain.
4. Helmet.
5. Water bottle.
6. Snacks.
7. Borough map or atlas.
8. Bicycle accessories: A horn and reflectors are standard safety features; toe clips, a rearview mirror, and a handlebar bag aren't necessary but can make the ride more enjoyable. An odometer can make it easier to follow tour directions.

Any bicycle will do for these tours. An increasingly popular choice for urban cycling is the all-terrain, or "mountain," bike (ATB). The ATB's heavy-duty frame and balloon tires can stand up to the ubiquitous potholes, patches, cracks, curbs, storm drains, and assorted debris of New York City streets. A delicate racer, on the other hand, will take a beating on some of these washboard roadways. A bike carrier for the car can help save some wear and tear on the equipment. The rear-mounted models are inexpensive, are simple to load, and fold easily to fit in any trunk.

The five boroughs of New York City offer some of the best bicycle touring opportunities found anywhere in the world. The topography is gentle, the climate is benign, and there are things to see and do *everywhere.*

1
Manhattan West Side Tour

Distance: 21 miles
Terrain: flat
Traffic: heavy

Climb aboard a World War II aircraft carrier complete with U.S. Navy fighter planes on deck; or sip espresso in a Bleecker Street coffeehouse once frequented by the likes of Jack Kerouac and Allen Ginsberg. From Ivy League tradition in the academic community of Morningside Heights to avant-garde art and music in SoHo and TriBeCa, Manhattan's West Side is a study in contrasts. Alongside the architectural landmarks of historic neighborhoods like Greenwich Village, Chelsea, and the Upper West Side are some of the most strikingly modern additions to the Manhattan skyline such as the World Trade Center, the futuristic Jacob K. Javits Convention Center, and Lincoln Center for the Performing Arts. Although there are plenty of milestones along this route, the interest lies not so much in the attractions themselves as in the rapid changes in ambience from one neighborhood to the next within a small geographical area. The hectic pace and raucous din of Times Square and the Garment District, for example, are all but forgotten only a few blocks away on the tranquil back streets of the West Village.

Begin the tour at the foot of Riverside Drive, at 72nd Street on the Upper West Side. Street parking should be fairly easy on a weekend morning. Avoid this tour on weekdays (other than holidays) unless you have the skill and determination to fight the world's worst traffic jams in Midtown and lower Manhattan. Sunday mornings are ideal for cycling in Manhattan.

Directions

0.0 Head north on Riverside Drive.

Easy pedaling on the Upper West Side's "scenic drive." Riverside Park and the Hudson River are on your left, and a wall of elegant apartment buildings and townhouses is on your right.

2.6 Turn RIGHT at West 122nd Street, opposite Grant's Tomb on your left.

Shortly before his death in 1885, Ulysses S. Grant, civil war hero and U.S. President from 1868 to 1876, requested burial in New York

City because his wife could not be interred with him at the U.S. Military Academy at West Point. The Roman-style mausoleum now overlooking the Hudson was the winning entry in an architectural competition held by the city to house the General's remains after his death. Inside the tomb lie the sarcophagi of Grant and his wife in a white marble and stained glass setting, along with an exhibit commemorating Grant's career. The General Grant National Memorial is open Wednesday through Sunday from 9:00 a.m. to 4:30 p.m. (1)

2.9 122nd Street becomes Morningside Drive as you cross Amsterdam Avenue. Morningside Drive curves to the right.

The campus of Columbia University lies a few blocks to the south and dominates the community of Morningside Heights. Most of the housing along Morningside Drive is associated with the University.

View of the Empire State Building from Tenth Avenue.

3.6 Turn LEFT at the foot of Morningside Drive, onto Cathedral Parkway.

Cathedral Parkway is named after the magnificent Cathedral of St. John the Divine, located on the northwest corner. Begun in 1892, the cathedral was about two-thirds completed when World War II broke out. Construction was halted, never to be resumed. Even in its unfinished state, St. John's is the largest Gothic cathedral in the world. In addition to its awesome nave, the building complex includes seven chapels, an impressive art collection, and a Biblical Garden containing only flora mentioned in the Bible. Open daily from 7:00 a.m. to 5:00 p.m. (The entrance is on Amsterdam Avenue, one block west of Morningside Drive.) (2)

4.2 Bear RIGHT at Frederick Douglass Circle and enter Central Park through an opening at the corner of Central Park West and the circle. Bear RIGHT at the stop sign, head onto West Drive, and follow the crowd of joggers and cyclists.

West Drive is closed to automobile traffic on weekends during the winter months and daily during spring and summer.

7.7 Exit Central Park at Seventh Avenue at the south end of the park and continue STRAIGHT down Seventh Avenue.

On your left at West 57th Street is New York's most famous musical landmark, Carnegie Hall. Its superb acoustics have attracted the

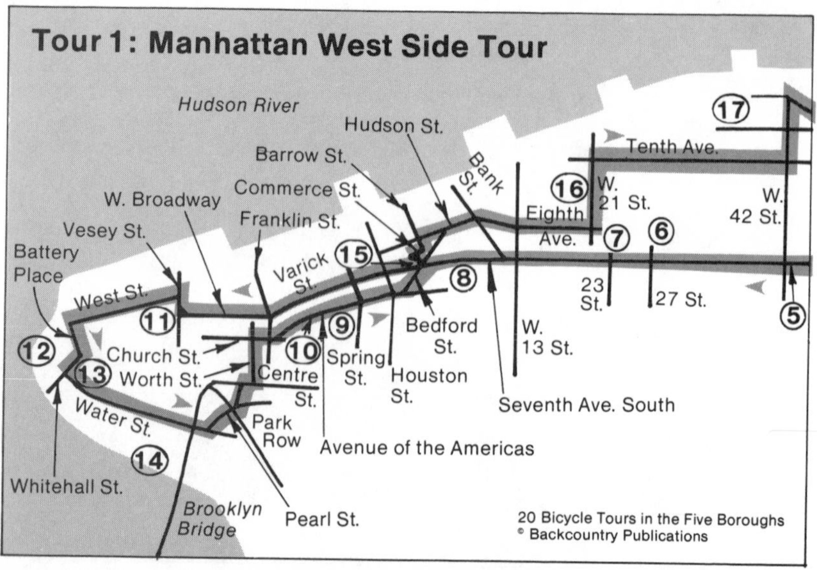

world's most gifted musicians for over a century. (3) Across from this musical landmark is a renowned culinary landmark, the Carnegie Delicatessen, at West 55th Street. It's New York's most popular Jewish deli and a long-time favorite of the Broadway show-biz crowd. (4)

8.4 At West 46th Street, keep to the right to stay on Seventh Avenue as Broadway and Seventh Avenue converge to form Times Square, on your left at West 42nd Street.

Although the triangle formed by the convergence of Broadway and Seventh Avenue still bears the name of the newspaper that erected its tower there at the turn of the century, the area today has little to do with news. This is the "adult entertainment" capital of the Western world, known for its crowds, flashy neon signs, and X-rated movies.

The Songwriters Hall of Fame, on the eighth floor of 1 Times Square, has a fascinating collection of musical memorabilia, including a display of the sheet music of every song that has ever won an Oscar. Open Monday through Saturday from 11:00 a.m. to 3:00 p.m., except major holidays. (5)

8.7 At West 40th Street, just below Times Square, Seventh Avenue becomes Fashion Avenue for a fifteen-block stretch as it passes through the Garment District.

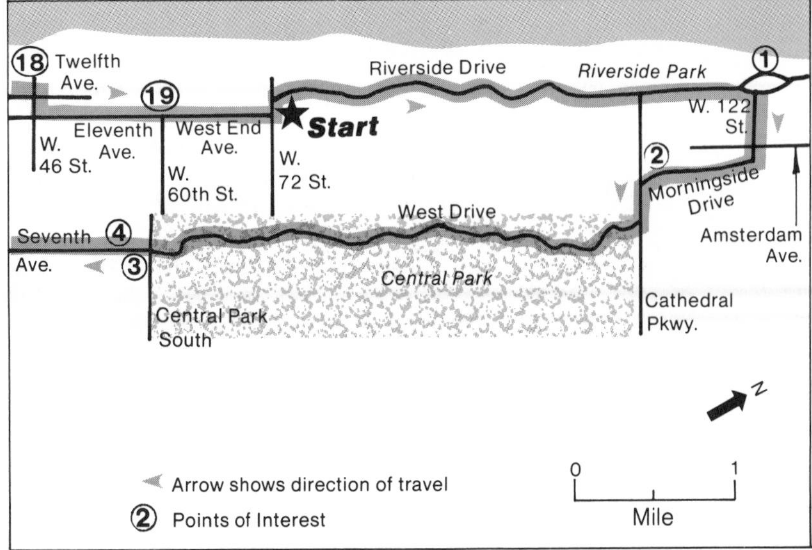

In the Garment District.

This area may look like a ghost town on weekends, but during the week New York's Garment District comes alive (and unbelievably congested) with the paraphernalia of the city's thriving "rag trade." Clothing racks, mannequins, pushcarts, and a myriad of trucks conveying everything from fur coats to pantyhose clog the avenue and side streets, creating the perpetual gridlock for which this colorful district is famous. The Fashion Institute of Technology, on your right at 27th Street at the edge of the district, trains many students for careers in New York's clothing industry. (6)

9.6 Continuing south on Seventh Avenue, detour half a block to the right at West 23rd Street for the Chelsea Hotel.

The literary and architectural landmark at 222 West 23rd Street is known both for the illustriousness of its guests and for its fanciful architecture. Mark Twain, Tennessee Williams, Sarah Bernhardt, and Yevgeny Yevtushenko are among the names of former residents listed on plaques at the hotel entrance. (7)

10.0 Seventh Avenue becomes Seventh Avenue South as you cross West 13th Street, entering Greenwich Village.

Sheridan Square, on your left at West 4th Street, is a convenient hub for exploring the winding streets, coffeehouses, and architectural anomalies of the West Village. While the Village is no longer the bohemian enclave of struggling artists and writers that it once was, it is still a symbol of unconventionality and social diversity to most New Yorkers. Controversial movements and avant-garde forms of art, music, and theater are still spawned here; and the Village's architectural heritage is forever preserved within the nation's second-largest Historic District. (8)

10.8 Seventh Avenue South becomes Varick Street as you cross Houston Street.

At Spring Street, detour three blocks to the left to visit SoHo. As recently as a decade ago, SoHo (for SOuth of HOuston) was a grimy industrial slum whose splendid cast-iron architecture was hidden among dusty warehouses and squalid sweatshops. In the most spectacular "architectural revival" in the city's history, the warehouses were converted to artists' lofts, with elegant shops and art galleries downstairs. Today, SoHo may well be the contemporary art capital of the world. But most striking to the casual visitor are the cast-iron facades that make SoHo the world's largest concentration of cast-iron architecture. Return to Varick Street and continue south. (9)

11.8 Varick Street merges into West Broadway at Franklin Street, a few blocks south of Canal Street.

TriBeCa (for TRIangle BElow CAnal) is in the early stages of a revival similar to SoHo's. Former warehouses and factories are being converted to artist's lofts, galleries, restaurants, and pubs. As Greenwich Village and SoHo become more respectable—and more expensive—many nonmainstream artists are seeking refuge below Canal Street. (10)

12.4 Turn RIGHT at the end of West Broadway, onto Vesey Street.

12.6 Turn LEFT at West Street, past the World Trade Center on your left.

On the morning of August 7, 1974, a French aerialist named Philippe Petit stretched a rope between the two 110-story towers of the World Trade Center and walked across it, creating a traffic-stopping spectacle for thousands of financial district office workers. Since their completion, the twin monoliths have inspired a number of daredevil feats. But they have failed to inspire architectural critics, many of whom resent their intrusion on the romantic lower Manhattan skyline. Nevertheless, tourists still love to visit the rooftop restaurant and observation deck for the breathtaking view, which takes in Manhattan, Long Island, and New Jersey. The six-building complex, the second tallest in the world, holds ten million square feet of office space, 104 elevators, and 21,800 windows that cannot be opened. (11)

Across from the World Trade Center is brand-new Battery Park City, a highly successful and aesthetically pleasing urban development project built on landfill.

13.2 Turn LEFT at the end of West Street, onto Battery Place, past Battery Park on your right.

Battery Park, at the southern tip of the island, owes its name to a row of cannons along the shorefront line that defended the young city's vulnerable coastline in the early 1800s. The Castle Clinton National Historic Monument, at the center of the park, was built in 1811 as a fort to defend the city during the War of 1812. For nearly two centuries since, it has served New York City well, first as a theater, then as an immigrant landing depot prior to Ellis Island, and finally as the home of the New York Aquarium before that institution moved to Coney Island in 1941. The fortress was slated for demolition in 1946 to make way for the construction of the Brooklyn Battery Tunnel. But Congress dubbed it a National Monument, thus saving the stone arena from oblivion. (12)

13.3 At the end of Battery Place, cross the cobblestone plaza in front of the former U.S. Custom House and turn RIGHT onto Whitehall Street.

Manhattan abounds in examples of the Beaux-Arts school of architecture, characterized by palatial dimensions, intricate facades, and monumental stone sculptures carved into and around the exterior. The U.S. Custom House, built in 1907, is the crown jewel of New York's Beaux-Arts buildings. The four limestone statues facing the plaza were sculpted by Daniel Chester French, of Lincoln Memorial fame. They represent the Four Continents—Asia, America, Europe, and Africa. The window arches above hold heads of the eight "races" of mankind. The interior of the building is equally imposing, with an elaborate vaulted ceiling, rich oak paneling, and brilliant wall frescoes. (13)

13.4 Turn LEFT at Water Street, past the Fraunces Tavern on your left at Broad Street.

It was here that George Washington bade farewell to his officers at the close of the Revolutionary War in 1783. Inside the tavern there's a museum specializing in the Revolutionary War period.

14.0 Stop at the South Street Seaport, on your right, opposite Fulton Street.

New York City owes her historic and commercial supremacy to her natural harbor and her proximity to the open sea. The South Street Seaport, a waterfront restoration centered around the old Fulton

Fish Market, is a celebration of New York's maritime heritage, with restored ships, piers, saloons, warehouses, shops, galleries, and lots of seafood—a good lunch stop. The museum and exhibition vessels are open daily from 11:00 a.m. to 5:00 p.m. (14)

14.0 **Continue north on Water Street.**

14.3 **Turn LEFT at Pearl Street, one block past the Brooklyn Bridge.**

14.5 **Bear LEFT as you cross Park Row, to stay on Pearl Street.**

14.7 **Turn RIGHT at Centre Street.**

14.8 **Take the first LEFT, at Worth Street.**

15.2 **Turn RIGHT at Church Street. Stay on the left side of the street.**

15.4 **Church Street curves left and becomes Avenue of the Americas at Franklin Street.**

16.1 **Bear LEFT as you cross Houston Street, onto Bedford Street.**

This typical West Village residential street, not much wider than an alley, is lined with early nineteenth-century houses, some of which are among the only remaining wood-frame houses in Manhattan. Number 75½, between Morton and Commerce, is "the narrowest house in the Village," at only 9.5 feet wide. It was briefly occupied by the poet Edna St. Vincent Millay during the 1920s. (15)

16.4 **Turn LEFT at Commerce Street, which bends sharply to the right. Turn LEFT at the end, onto Barrow Street. Take the first RIGHT at Hudson Street, which becomes Eighth Avenue at Bank Street.**

17.1 **Turn LEFT at West 21st Street.**

A typical Chelsea street, West 21st Street is lined with the Greek Revival and Italianate rowhouses for which this neighborhood was designated a Historic District. Note the row of adjoining wooden houses on the northwest corner as you cross Ninth Avenue, opposite the austere General Theological Seminary. (16)

17.6 **Turn RIGHT at Tenth Avenue, past the Empire Diner on your right at West 22nd Street.**

The all-American roadside diner has all but disappeared from this cosmopolitan city. The Empire Diner, opened in 1943, is an authentic—though updated—relic of that American institution.

18.9 **Turn LEFT at West 42nd Street. As you cross Eleventh Avenue, detour 5 blocks to the left to visit the brand-new Jacob K. Javits Convention Center.**

The futuristic glass-enclosed space was completed in 1986 to replace the outmoded Coliseum as New York's trade show and exhibition center. The four-block-long center consists of 61,000 glass panels and 100,000 square feet of skylights. (17)

Return to West 42nd Street and continue west.

19.4 Cross Twelfth Avenue and turn RIGHT for the Intrepid Aircraft Carrier and Sea-Air-Space Museum.

The sight of a nine hundred-foot World War II aircraft carrier, complete with U.S. Navy fighter planes on board its flight deck, may not turn heads in San Diego or Norfolk. But one hardly expects to see a battleship berthed alongside the cruise ships and ocean liners on Manhattan's West Side. Nevertheless, the U.S.S. *Intrepid,* which saw battle in the mid-Pacific, Korea, and Vietnam, has been a big hit with New Yorkers since the city acquired the retired vessel from the Navy in 1981 and converted it to a museum. The opportunity to climb aboard and view exhibits on naval aviation and space-age technology is worth the $5 admission fee. Open daily from 10:00 a.m. to 7:00 p.m. (18)

Leaving the *Intrepid,* cross Twelfth Avenue and head east on West 46th Street.

19.6 Take the first LEFT at Eleventh Avenue.

The next twenty blocks or so are lined with an uninspiring array of auto dealerships, repair shops, garages, and parking lots. This neighborhood was once a part of the notorious Hell's Kitchen, a district of slaughterhouses, freightyards, and glue factories that bordered the Hudson River Railroad running down Eleventh Avenue. The elimination of the grade-level railroad in the 1940s led to physical and social changes that are still taking place now. (19)

Eleventh Avenue becomes West End Avenue at West 60th Street.

20.9 Turn LEFT at West 72nd Street, back to the starting point at Riverside Drive.

Bicycle Shops

Bicycle Habitat, 194 Seventh Avenue (between 21st and 22nd Streets), Manhattan (212-691-2783)

Canal Street Bicycle, 417 Canal Street (at Grand Street), Manhattan (212-334-8000)

Toga Bike Shop, 110 West End Avenue (at 66th Street), Manhattan (212-799-9625)

2
Across 110th Street

Distance: 14 miles
Terrain: hilly
Traffic: moderate

For some New Yorkers, 110th Street, or Central Park North, is an imaginary boundary that divides lower Manhattan from the borough's "forbidden" upper reaches of Harlem and beyond. Although some upper Manhattan communities well deserve their reputations as high-crime, blighted neighborhoods, the whole truth is that those who never venture past the north end of Central Park are missing some of the most fascinating and historically significant parts of the city. Several Historic Districts containing some of the most distinguished landmarks in the borough are located here, as are two architecturally (and academically) outstanding college campuses, a National Historic Monument, a number of unique museums, and many other points of interest. Cyclists will appreciate the area's wide boulevards and lighter traffic as compared with lower Manhattan. Those apprehensive about pedaling in these neglected but highly engrossing parts of the city can cycle with friends on a busy afternoon and take comfort in the safety of numbers.

The tour begins at West 81st Street and Central Park West, in front of the American Museum of Natural History. The route takes you uptown, across 110th Street into Morningside Heights, Harlem, and Hamilton Heights before turning around at one of the city's most cherished institutions, Yankee Stadium, just over the Macomb's Dam Bridge in the Bronx. As the names of these communities suggest, this is a rather hilly tour.

Directions

0.0 Head uptown on Central Park West.

1.6 Turn LEFT at Frederick Douglass Circle (at West 110th Street), onto Cathedral Parkway.

1.8 Take the second RIGHT onto Morningside Drive, uphill, past the Cathedral of St. John the Divine and Columbia University housing on your left.

2.5 Turn RIGHT at Amsterdam Avenue.

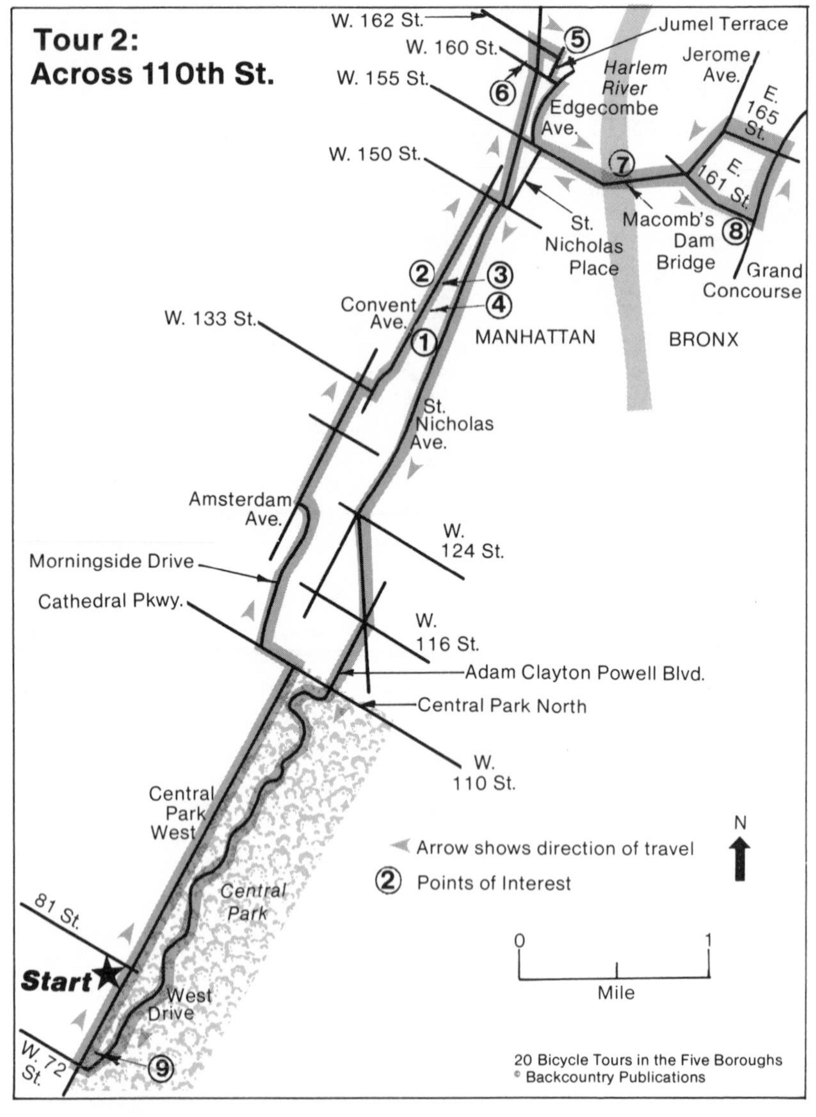

3.1 Turn RIGHT at West 133rd Street.

3.2 Turn LEFT at the end, onto Convent Avenue, and pass through the campus of City College at West 138th Street.

In 1952, the Academy and Convent of the Sacred Heart (established in 1841) moved to Westchester County, leaving behind its complex of cathedrallike buildings and courtyards. The city bought the property and turned it over to City College (established in 1849), now part of the City University of New York (CUNY). The college was originally free to all city residents who could pass its entrance exams. At the turn of the century the student body consisted almost entirely of Jews from Eastern European families. Today the enrollment is largely Black and Hispanic. The university, although no longer free, is still considered an educational outlet for aspiring minority groups. (1)

Continue STRAIGHT uptown on Convent Avenue.

Just beyond the City College campus, at 287 Convent Avenue, stands the two-story yellow frame house that was built in 1802 as a country home for Alexander Hamilton and his family. Hamilton, who helped draft the U.S. Constitution and served as the nation's first Secretary of the Treasury, lived here until the end of his life in 1804, when he was fatally wounded in a duel with his political enemy, Aaron Burr. The Hamilton Grange National Historic Monument is open Monday through Friday from 9:00 a.m. to 4:30 p.m. Admission is free. (2)

One block to the right of Convent Avenue is Hamilton Terrace, part of the Hamilton Heights Historic District, an enclave of picturesque brownstones, rowhouses, and churches that was given landmark status in 1974. The charm and quality of the housing in this area have traditionally attracted professors and staff from the neighboring college. For museum buffs, Aunt Len's Doll and Toy Museum at 6 Hamilton Terrace has a collection of nearly three thousand dolls, ranging from miniature replicas of Sonny and Cher to brightly costumed ethnic dolls from every corner of the world. Admission is by appointment—call ahead: 212-281-4143. (3,4)

Continue STRAIGHT uptown on Convent Avenue.

4.5 Turn RIGHT at West 150th Street, then turn LEFT immediately, onto St. Nicholas Avenue.

5.2 Turn RIGHT at West 162nd Street, then take another RIGHT immediately, onto cobblestoned Jumel Terrace.

Just up the road from Alexander Hamilton's country home stands another historic building that, ironically, was occupied for several years by the man who took Hamilton's life, Aaron Burr. The Morris-Jumel Mansion, on your left in tiny Roger Morris Park, is one of the city's few remaining pre-Revolutionary buildings. The mansion was built in 1765 as a summer residence for a wealthy British colonel and his wife. During the Revolution it served for a time as Washington's headquarters because its high site offered views of both the

Hamilton Grange Historic Monument, Upper Manhattan.

Harlem and the Hudson rivers. The city acquired the property in 1903 and in 1907 opened a museum there under the auspices of the Daughters of the American Revolution. The interior is furnished with authentic period pieces, including a bed and chairs that once belonged to Napoleon. Open Tuesday through Sunday from 10:00 a.m. to 4:00 p.m. Admission is $1. (5)

Directly across from the mansion, on what was once the estate's carriage drive, is an alley framed by two rows of beautifully restored wooden rowhouses built for workers in 1882. Sylvan Terrace, along with the mansion and the surrounding limestone rowhouses, was given landmark status in 1970, as part of the Jumel Terrace Historic District. (6)

From Jumel Terrace, turn LEFT at West 160th Street, then RIGHT at Edgecombe Avenue, downhill.

5.8 Turn LEFT at the bottom of the hill, onto West 155th Street, which will

take you to the Macomb's Dam Bridge, over the Harlem River and into the Bronx.

This graceful steel span, one of eleven bridges connecting Manhattan with the Bronx over the Harlem River, owes its name to a dam and toll bridge that stood on this site for fifteen years during the early 1800s. A local citizen named Robert Macomb had built the dam to harness the river's power to run a mill, but he thereby obstructed shipping and turned the river upstream into a mill pond. In 1838, an angry mob destroyed the dam with picks and shovels to restore the river's navigability.

Go slow. Both the roadway and the walkway of the bridge are in poor condition, with warped metal plates and gaps between sections. (7)

The bridge curves to the left as it crosses the Major Deegan Expressway. Do not get off the bridge at the first exit; continue all the way to the end.

6.5 Coming off the bridge, turn RIGHT at West 161st Street, past Yankee Stadium on your right.

In 1923, Yankee owner Jacob Ruppert designed and built this stadium with a short right field to accommodate his left-handed star player, Babe Ruth. The short right field helped Ruth set his home-run record. Joe DiMaggio and Mickey Mantle are among the other players who made baseball history at this South Bronx landmark. (8)

6.8 Turn LEFT at Grand Concourse.

7.3 Turn LEFT at West 165th Street, down a steep hill.

7.6 Turn LEFT at the end, onto Jerome Avenue, which will take you back to the Macomb's Dam Bridge into Manhattan. Continue on the bridge to the end, which will put you on West 155th Street, uphill.

8.6 Turn LEFT at the top of the hill, onto St. Nicholas *Avenue* (not St. Nicholas Place).

10.2 Bear LEFT at West 124th Street to stay on St. Nicholas Avenue.

10.6 Bear RIGHT at West 116th Street, onto Adam Clayton Powell Boulevard.

11.0 Cross Central Park North at the end and continue STRAIGHT into Central Park, bearing RIGHT onto West Drive.

13.4 Exit the park at West 72nd Street.

To your left as you exit the park is Strawberry Fields, the lovely garden commissioned by the widow of John Lennon in memory of the former Beatle, who was assassinated in 1980 in front of his apartment building, the luxurious Dakota, on the northwest corner of West 72nd Street and Central Park West. (10)

13.6 Turn RIGHT onto Central Park West, back to the starting point at West 81st Street.

If you still have some time and energy left, the American Museum of Natural History has a phenomenal collection of fossils, minerals, gems, meteorites, dinosaurs, and other specimens pertaining to the evolution of our planet. The Hayden Planetarium next door features the "Sky Theatre," in which celestial phenomena are projected onto the interior of a huge overhead dome. Open Monday through Friday from 10:00 a.m. to 4:45 p.m; and Saturday and Sunday from 10:00 a.m. to 5:00 p.m. Admission to the Museum is by donation. Admission to the planetarium is free if you enter through the Museum; otherwise it is $3.75 for adults and $2.00 for children between the ages of two and twelve.

Bicycle Shops

Bicycle Renaissance, 491 Amsterdam Avenue (between 83rd and 84th Streets), Manhattan (212-362-3388)

Party Riders Bicycle Shop, 575 Grand Concourse (between 149th and 150th Streets), The Bronx (212-585-7964)

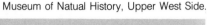

Museum of Natual History, Upper West Side.

3
Island Hopping

Distance: 18.5 miles
Terrain: flat
Traffic: moderate

A hundred years ago, the City of New York dealt with criminals, lunatics, the infectiously ill, the destitute, and other "misfits" by exiling them to one of the islands that dot the East River between Manhattan and the outer boroughs. Consequently, those islands long held little more than a forbidding collection of penal institutions, insane asylums, poorhouses, hospitals, and potter's fields. Although the crumbling ruins of some of these institutions remain, the islands present a much brighter picture today. Roosevelt Island (formerly Welfare Island) is the site of a successful middle-income housing development. Ward's and Randall's Islands consist mainly of attractive parklands with recreational and athletic facilities, a stadium, and a few official buildings. If you're curious about the city's offshore territories, here's a chance to explore. Following a dramatic ride over the waters of Hell Gate, you'll visit the islands, pedal the length of Manhattan's "Museum Mile," and finish with a spin around a historic Queens neighborhood.

Officially, the islands belong to the borough of Manhattan, but they are easily reached from Queens. This "island-hopping" tour begins in Astoria at the foot of the Triborough Bridge, at the Municipal Parking Lot at 29th Street and Hoyt Avenue *South.* Please pay close attention to the directions, as much of the route, particularly on the islands, follows a maze of paths and unmarked roadways. Ward's Island is presently the site of a shelter for homeless men, a drug treatment facility, and a psychiatric hospital. Though security is tight on the island, women are advised not to ride alone on Ward's and Randall's Islands.

0.0 Leaving the parking lot, cross Hoyt Avenue South and locate the stairway, about fifty yards to the left, that will take you up onto the bike path of the Triborough Bridge.

Hundreds of shipwrecks are believed to lie beneath the treacherous waters of Hell Gate, the channel that leads to the Atlantic Ocean, via Long Island Sound, from the East River. The Y-shaped Triborough Bridge, which spans the channel, was designed to connect the three boroughs of Manhattan, Queens, and the Bronx. To your left is

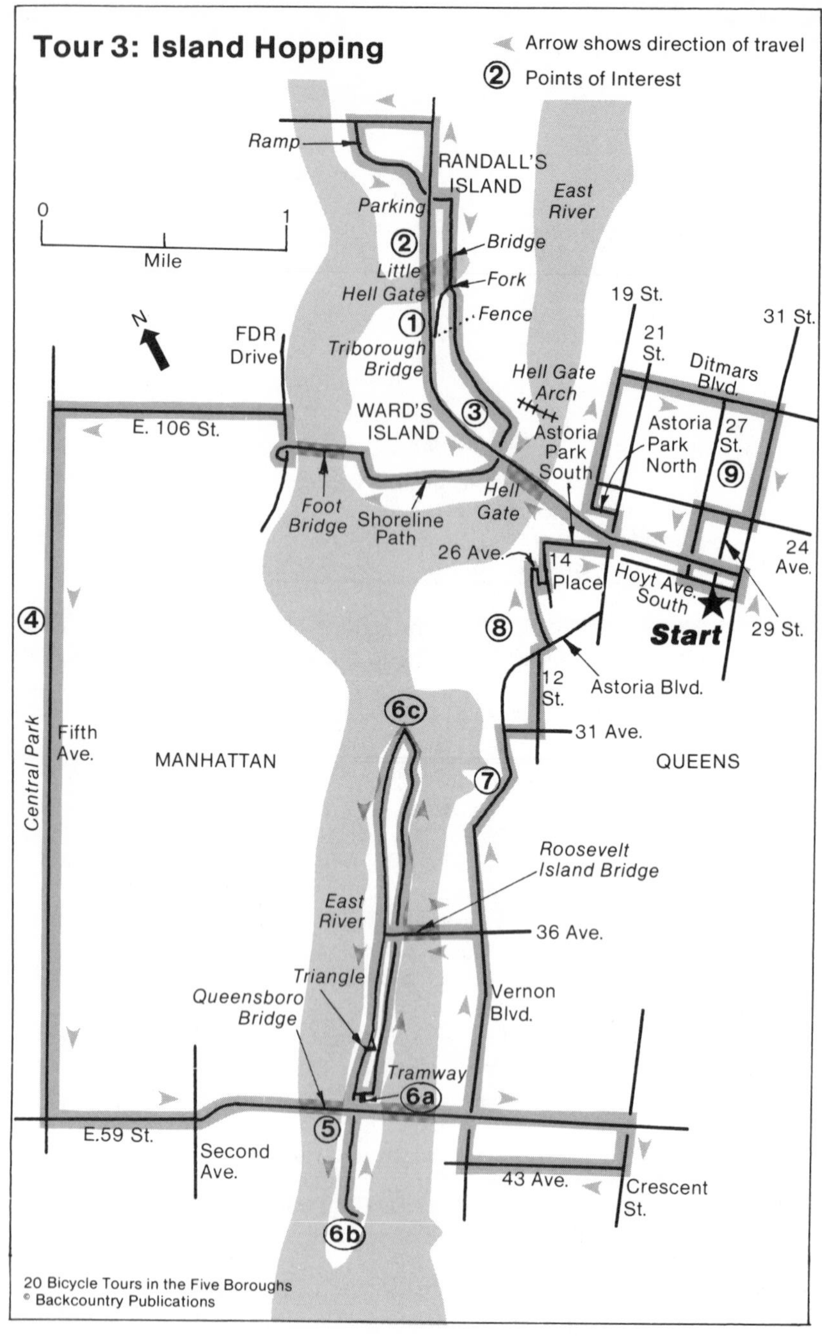

a splendid view of the Midtown skyline; to your right, a view of the Hell Gate Arch, the handsome railroad bridge that provides New

York City with a direct rail link to New England and the rest of the Northeast Corridor. (1)

1.8 At the bottom of the ramp coming off the bridge onto Randall's Island, turn LEFT across the parking lot, then RIGHT onto the unmarked roadway. Follow the signs to Ward's Island.

The completion of the Triborough Bridge in 1936 made Randall's Island accessible and paved the way for its development as a park and recreational facility. John J. Downing Stadium is used for summer concerts, athletic events, and the San Juan Festival in June. (2)

Just before you come to a bridge over landfill onto Ward's Island, look for the New York City Fire Department Training Center on your left. It is not open to the public, but you can glimpse part of a "mock city" that is meant to be set on fire and extinguished as part of the firemen's training.

2.0 Cross the bridge onto Ward's Island.

Ward's Island used to be separated from Randall's Island by a channel called "Little Hell Gate." The two bodies of land have since been joined by landfill. Ward's Island is mostly a recreation area, but it is also home to some city and state psychiatric facilities. (3)

2.3 Bear LEFT at the fork, passing a water pollution control plant on your left.

2.5 You will come to a chain-link fence. If the gate is locked, look for the opening for pedestrians to the right of the gate. After passing through the gate, make the first LEFT and continue STRAIGHT, downhill, toward the water.

2.8 Bear RIGHT along the shoreline, passing underneath the Triborough Bridge and proceeding along the southern shore of the island.

3.4 Turn LEFT, onto the narrow blue-green footbridge that takes you over the East River into Manhattan. Stay on the bridge in order to cross Franklin Delano Roosevelt (FDR) Drive.

3.7 Coming off the footbridge, turn north (uptown) along the highway and continue for three blocks to East 106th Street, then turn LEFT there.

4.7 Turn LEFT at the end of 106th, onto Fifth Avenue.

The stretch of Fifth Avenue from East 106th Street south to East 79th Street has acquired the nickname "Museum Mile" because of the nearly unbroken row of cultural institutions that lines the avenue for more than twenty blocks. Some are free; others charge a small admission fee. Bike racks are usually available. Some of the more prominent museums are:

El Museo del Barrio, 105th Street. Free.
Museum of the City of New York, 103rd Street. Free.

International Center of Photography, 95th Street.
The Jewish Museum, 92nd Street.
Cooper-Hewitt Museum (design), 91st Street.
Solomon R. Guggenheim Museum (art), 89th Street.
Metropolitan Museum of Art, 82nd Street.
Goethe House (German), 82nd Street. Free. (4)

6.2 Continue STRAIGHT along Fifth Avenue.

7.0 Turn LEFT at 59th Street.

7.5 Cross Second Avenue and follow the bicycle signs to the outer roadway of the Queensboro Bridge.

The southbound outer roadway is usually closed to traffic and reserved for bicycles and pedestrians. At other times the Traffic Department operates a "bikebus," taking cyclists and their bikes across the bridge during peak traffic hours. Look for a brown van trailing a sort of flatbed wagon behind.

The Queensboro, or 59th Street, Bridge, with its intricate steel latticework, is a widely recognized symbol of the Big Apple and has appeared as a romantic backdrop in many a Hollywood film set in New York. Poets, songwriters, and TV producers have evoked the image of this ornate span in their works. (5)

8.9 Coming off the bridge, turn RIGHT at the stop sign, onto Crescent Street.

9.1 Turn RIGHT at 43rd Avenue.

A short but uncomfortable stretch of cobblestones is coming up as you cross 21st Street.

9.6 Turn RIGHT at the end of 43rd, onto Vernon Boulevard.

10.3 Turn LEFT at 36th Street, onto the Roosevelt Island Bridge. Follow the "Island Access" sign, down a circular ramp.

10.8 Turn LEFT at the bottom of the ramp, into the main residential area of Roosevelt Island.

Once a place of banishment for criminals and madmen, the former Welfare Island became the site of a successful experiment in urban planning in 1975. It is now home to a community of about six thousand residents of mixed economic background. (6)

11.1 Bear RIGHT at the triangle, past the tramway station and underneath the Queensboro Bridge.

Relics of the island's past still turn up among the high-rises. The Blackwell Farmhouse, at the triangle just beyond the housing development, is the restored clapboard dwelling of the family that owned

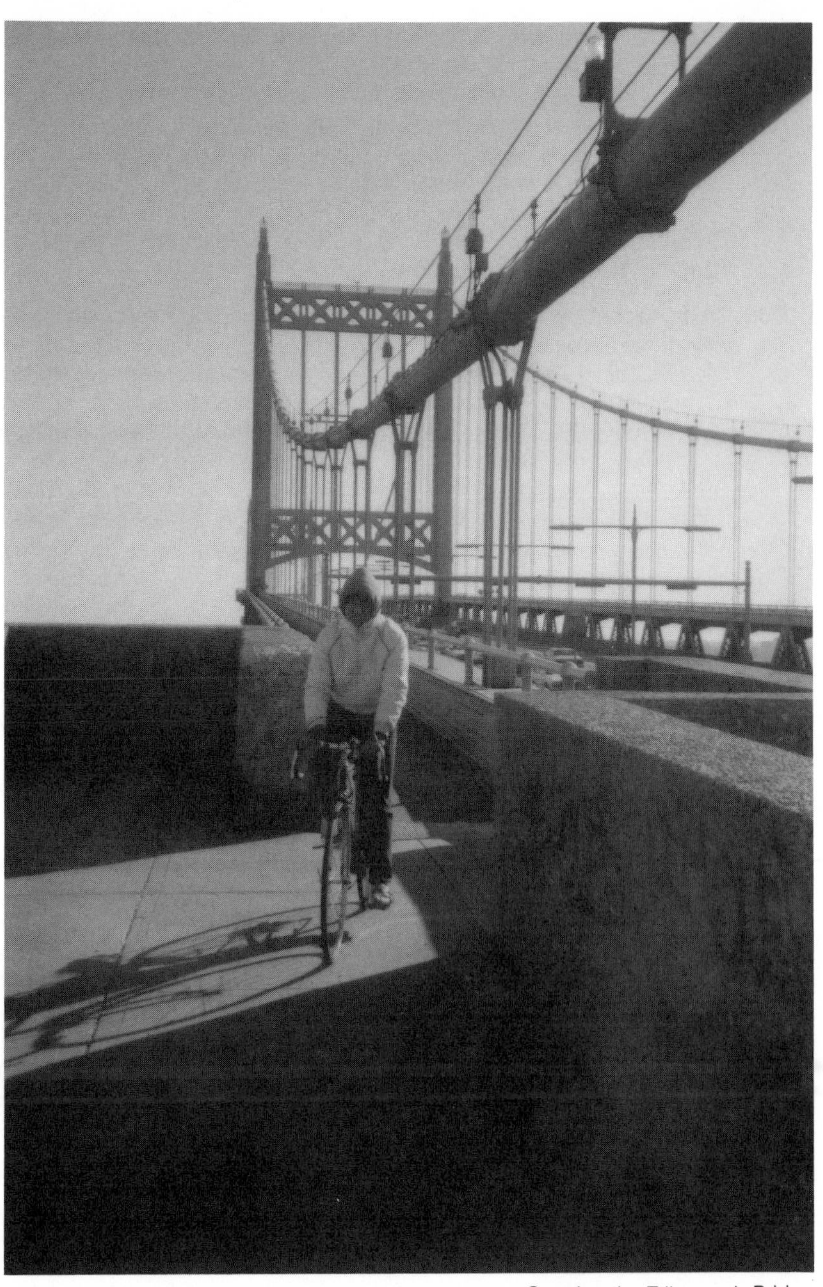

Crossing the Triborough Bridge.

and farmed this island from the late 1600s until 1828, when they sold the land to the city.

The aerial tramway is the city's innovative answer to the problem of access to the island from Manhattan. At one time, pedestrians could step off the middle of the Queensboro Bridge, onto the eighth floor of an office tower situated on the island and descend by elevator to ground level. (6a)

Continue along the East River, past the Goldwater Hospital for Chronic Diseases, on your left.

11.7 At the end of the river promenade, turn around and retrace your path back to the tramway station.

The ruins of a former prison hospital and smallpox infirmary attest to the island's past as a place of confinement and quarantine. (6b)

Just *past* the tramway station, turn RIGHT, then LEFT at the end, to ride along the eastern shore of the island. Follow the shoreline for about 1.3 miles to Lighthouse Park, at the northern tip of the island.

The fifty-foot landmark lighthouse is rumored to have been built by an inmate of a nearby lunatic asylum who feared an invasion by the British. A bizarre inscription carved into the stone gives some credibility to the legend. (6c)

13.6 Swing around the lighthouse, onto the western shore of the island, and return to the Roosevelt Island Bridge.

14.4 Turn LEFT onto the bridge and head up the circular ramp and back into Queens.

14.9 Turn LEFT at the foot of the bridge, onto Vernon Boulevard.

Watch for the Socrates Sculpture Space, on your left opposite Broadway. What looks at first glance like just a junkyard is actually an exhibit of modern sculpture displayed on a tract of city-owned land against the backdrop of the East River and the Manhattan skyline. Stop and take a look. Some prominent artists are represented here, and the work is fascinating. The exhibit is free and open till dusk. (7)

Continue STRAIGHT on Vernon Boulevard, going north.

15.5 Turn RIGHT at 31st *Avenue* (not 31st Drive), just past the Sculpture Space.

15.6 Take the first LEFT at 12th Street.

15.9 Bear LEFT, crossing Astoria Boulevard, to stay on 12th Street.

This part of Astoria is an enclave of faded grandeur, containing a number of former mansions and eccentric "country" homes that have survived from around the early 1800s, when the area was a fashionable summer colony and the center of a thriving shipping industry. (8)

16.1 **Turn RIGHT at 26th Avenue.**

16.2 **Turn RIGHT at the end, then LEFT, to stay on 26th Avenue.**

16.3 Turn LEFT at 14th *Place.*

16.4 **Turn RIGHT at the end, onto Astoria Park South.**

16.6 **Take the first LEFT, at 21st Street.**

16.7 **Take the first LEFT, at Astoria Park North.**

16.8 **Take the first RIGHT, at 19th Street.**

17.1 **Turn RIGHT, onto Ditmars Boulevard.**

17.5 Turn RIGHT, onto 31st Street.

In this part of Queens, restaurants serve moussaka and stuffed grape leaves; bars are *tavernas;* and coffeehouses offer a thick black brew with sweet baklava. This section of Astoria is nicknamed Little Athens and is said to hold the largest number of Greek nationals outside of Athens. In addition to the restaurants, there are Greek movies, gift shops, groceries, and nightclubs with belly dancers. For the less adventurous, the Neptune Diner at 31st Street and Astoria Boulevard features standard American fare in addition to authentic Greek dishes. (9)

18.0 **Turn RIGHT at 24th Avenue.**

18.2 **Turn LEFT at 27th Street, which will take you back to the municipal parking lot at Hoyt Avenue South.**

Bicycle Shops

Long Island City Cycles, 42-21 Broadway (just over the Queensboro Bridge), Long Island City (718-728-1447)

Pedal Pusher, 1306 Second Avenue (between 68th and 69th Streets), Manhattan (212-288-5592)

4
Bronx Safari

Distance: 12 miles
Terrain: rolling
Traffic: light

See giant tortoises and exotic reptiles in their natural habitats; wander through forty acres of virgin hemlock forest; gaze upon an ancient river gorge and waterfall. Is it the African plain? No, it's our own Bronx Park, with its two world-famous institutions, the Bronx Zoo and Botanical Garden! Unlike the bike tours atypical of the Bronx—"The Other Bronx" and "Gold Coast"—this central Bronx ride takes in the borough's most widely known and best-loved attractions, as well as some of its most characteristic neighborhoods. In addition to the venerable zoo and Botanical Garden, there are Fordham University and the Grand Concourse, Arthur Avenue (the Bronx's Little Italy) and Pelham Parkway. You hardly need a guide for a portion of the ride—about one-third of the route follows a city-designated bikeway that winds around and through Bronx Park and along the Pelham and Mosholu parkways. Both parkways, with their bikeways, were designed as part of a scheme to link the borough's major parks through a system of luxurious thoroughfares. Whether or not the plan succeeded, the bikeways provide some very pleasant traffic-free cycling. Though it is short on miles, this tour is long on leisurely attractions, so allow plenty of time to explore these *nationally* acclaimed Bronx wonders.

The ride begins in a quiet residential section of the borough, near the foot of Pelham Parkway at Eastchester Road. Drivers, take the Hutchinson River Parkway to Pelham Parkway North and from there, proceed to Eastchester Road.

Directions

0.0 Head north along Pelham Parkway, on the bicycle path adjacent to the parkway.

The bikeway is smooth and well maintained and runs for several miles along this wide, tree-lined boulevard. Pelham Parkway was the first effort in a master plan to link the large parks of the Bronx by luxurious thoroughfares; others include Mosholu Parkway and the Grand Concourse. With its broad expanses of lawns and trees, its

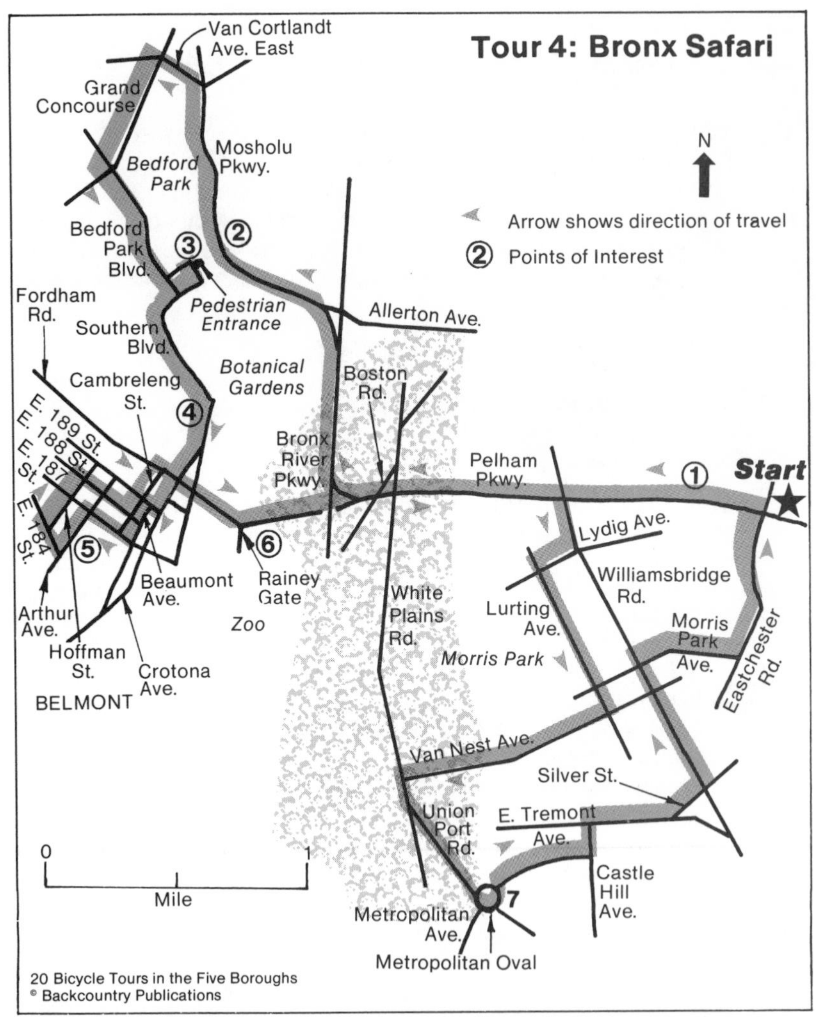

rock outcroppings, and its bridle and bicycle paths, Pelham Parkway is a park in itself. (1)

1.1 After crossing Boston Road, bear RIGHT at the sign indicating the Bronx River Parkway North. You will pick up another bicycle path at the southwest corner of Bronx Park East.

After passing a comfort station, playground, and ballfield on your right, you will find yourself heading north along the Bronx River Parkway.

1.8 Turn LEFT at the first traffic light, onto Allerton Avenue.

Watch out for fast-moving traffic. After passing the highway exit ramp, pick up the bikepath on your right.

2.4 Turn RIGHT at the next traffic light onto the bikeway of Mosholu Parkway North, past the 52nd Precinct house on your right.

This fanciful building is described by the American Institute of Architects as "Tuscan villa-inspired." With its terra-cotta clock faces and deep eaves, the landmark building is one of the most striking examples of the Romantic architecture that is prevalent in the Bedford Park section of the Bronx. (2)

3.0 Turn LEFT at Van Cortlandt Avenue East.

3.2 Turn LEFT at the Grand Concourse.

Be sure to turn onto the southbound service road, and not onto the main road.

3.6 Turn LEFT at Bedford Park Boulevard, going downhill.

The Bedford Park section of the Bronx, although it is somewhat rundown at present, is considered a treasury of art deco architecture. These buildings are contained in a hilly enclave east of the Grand Concourse.

4.1 Turn LEFT at the end, for about 0.1 mile, into the pedestrian entrance to the Botanical Garden.

The New York Botanical Garden includes 250 acres of garden and lawn, a conservatory, an arboretum, and wilderness. Some of the highlights are a nineteenth-century snuff mill built by the Lorillard family, of tobacco fame; forty acres of uncut woodland, the only virgin forest remaining in New York City; a "glass fairyland" of landmark greenhouses; and the Bronx River gorge, a wildernesslike setting where the effects of the Wisconsin Glacier are visible. Admission to the grounds is free, but some of the individual attractions charge admission. Open daily from dawn to dusk. Bike racks and an attendant's booth are located just inside the entrance. (3)

4.2 Leaving the Botanical Garden, turn LEFT onto Southern Boulevard. Southern Boulevard curves left, past the campus of Fordham University on your right.

Fordham is one of the largest Catholic universities in the country and one of the city's venerable institutions. Visitors are allowed in to see the administration building—originally an 1836 Greek Revival mansion known as Rose Hill—and the imposing yet picturesque Keating Hall (the building with the clock tower and the incongruous antenna). The entrance to the university is directly across from the main entrance to the Botanical Garden. Incidentally, the university takes its name from the community, not vice versa. (4)

Leaving the university, turn RIGHT onto Southern Boulevard.

5.0 Bear RIGHT just past the campus, onto Crotona Avenue.

5.2 Turn RIGHT at East 189th Street. Take the first LEFT, onto Beaumont Avenue.

5.4 Turn RIGHT at East 187th Street.

5.5 Turn LEFT at Arthur Avenue.

The neighborhood of Belmont—also called the Arthur Avenue district—is the Bronx's Little Italy, a cohesive Italian-American community best known for its gastronomic delights. People come here from all over the city to shop for freshly baked Italian breads, salami, olive oil, fresh fish, and dairy products from the open-air produce and seafood stalls. Some people say Belmont is more authentically Italian than Manhattan's Little Italy. While Manhattan's Little Italy is slowly being engulfed by Chinatown, Belmont has been fighting off encroaching urban blight from the South and West Bronx. Thanks to the determination of its citizens, the neighborhood is a haven of stability, even though it is bordered by some of the city's worst slums.

You might want to stop in at Dominick's, on Arthur Avenue, a no-frills restaurant without a menu that serves some of the most authentic dishes in the district—mostly vast platters of pasta and sauces—at reasonable prices. (5)

5.7 Turn RIGHT at East 184th Street. Take the first RIGHT at Hoffman Street.

6.0 Turn RIGHT at 188th Street.

6.2 Turn LEFT at Cambreleng Street.

6.3 Turn RIGHT at the end, onto Fordham Road.

6.7 Turn RIGHT into the Rainey Memorial Gates of the Bronx Zoo.

Even if you don't choose to visit the zoo, stop for a moment to admire the beautiful bronze gates, an architectural landmark sculpted in 1934 by Paul Manship, depicting a "tree of life" with twenty-two full-sized animals.

The Bronx Zoo, or the New York Zoological Gardens, has only 252 acres and may seem cramped compared with some of the more modern zoos in other cities. But it remains one of the world's most famous menageries. Over three hundred species of birds and other animals live in simulated natural habitats. There are African plains, South American pampas, North American buffalo plains, an elk forest, a wolf wood, and some indoor exhibits replicating rain-forest environments. Open Monday through Saturday from 10:00 a.m. to 5:00 p.m.; Sunday until 5:30 p.m. Admission is free on Tuesday, Wednesday, and Thursday. $2.50 on other days. (6)

Leaving the Rainey gates, turn RIGHT onto Fordham Road, which becomes Pelham Parkway as you cross White Plains Road.

Watch out for fast-moving, aggressive traffic. Around here you will encounter the only appreciable traffic on this tour.

7.8 **Turn RIGHT at Williamsbridge Road.**

7.9 **Take the first RIGHT, at Lydig Avenue.**

8.0 **Turn LEFT at Lurting Avenue.**

8.6 **Turn RIGHT at Van Nest Avenue.**

In the New York Zoological Garden.

9.3 Turn LEFT at White Plains Road.

9.4 Take the first LEFT, onto Unionport Road, crossing over a green bridge.

Continue on Unionport, through the Parkchester Housing Project, until you come to the Metropolitan Oval, a large grassy circle with a fountain in the middle. This prewar housing development, built between 1938 and 1942, is considered a triumph of urban planning because of its human scale, its landscaping, its curving roads, and its shopping center. The terra-cotta ornaments that adorn the building are hard to miss. Don't miss the very amusing sculpture at the center of the Metropolitan Oval (named after the Metropolitan Life Insurance Company, which built and administered the project for thirty years. (7)

9.8 Leaving the Metropolitan Oval, head *east* on Metropolitan Avenue.

Make sure the building numbers are increasing. If they are not, go back and pick up Metropolitan Avenue on the other side of the oval.

10.1 Turn LEFT at Castle Hill Avenue.

10.2 Turn RIGHT at East Tremont Avenue.

10.4 Bear LEFT at Silver Street, on your left opposite Overing Street.

10.6 Take the second LEFT, at Williamsbridge Road.

11.1 Turn RIGHT at Morris Park Avenue.

11.5 Turn LEFT at Eastchester Road, which takes you back to the starting point at Pelham Parkway.

Bicycle Shops

Cycle Medics, 2245 White Plains Road (near Boston Road), Williamsbridge (212-231-5546)

Westchester Bicycle Pro Shop, 2611 Westchester Avenue (212-409-1114)

Square Sport Shop, 136 Westchester Square (212-823-7474)

5
Gold Coast

Distance: 13 miles
Terrain: hilly
Traffic: moderate

Some of the finest real estate in the five boroughs can be found on a narrow strip of land in the north Bronx, extending from Broadway, west to the banks of the Hudson River. A trio of communities there are among the most scenic in the borough. The exclusive residential community of Riverdale is an area of winding, hilly streets, romantic views of the Hudson, and meticulously landscaped estates, including the world-famous garden and environmental center, Wave Hill. Riverdale was nicknamed "Gold Coast" in the early part of this century because of the many affluent and influential people who resided there. Just south of this enclave are the neighborhoods of Spuyten Duyvil, overlooking the confluence of the Harlem and Hudson rivers, and Kingsbridge, at the southwest corner of Van Cortlandt Park. The presence of three college campuses, including the architecturally striking College of Mount St. Vincent at the north end of Riverdale, enhances the distinction of this corner of the Bronx.

The tour begins on busy Broadway, at the corner of West 251st Street, on the western edge of Van Cortlandt Park. It turns west into surprisingly bucolic surroundings. This is a difficult ride in terms of terrain and road conditions. Traffic is light in Riverdale, but steep hills and rough, pitted roads present a challenge in places. Yet it is precisely these inconveniences that give the locality its charm.

Directions

0.0 **Head north (uptown) on Broadway.**

1.0 **Turn LEFT at West 261st Street, uphill.**

1.6 **Turn RIGHT at the end of West 261st Street, into the campus of the College of Mount St. Vincent.**

The campus is worth a visit for its bizarre architecture, beautifully landscaped grounds, and lovely views of the Hudson River. The Sisters of Charity, who operate the college, purchased the site from

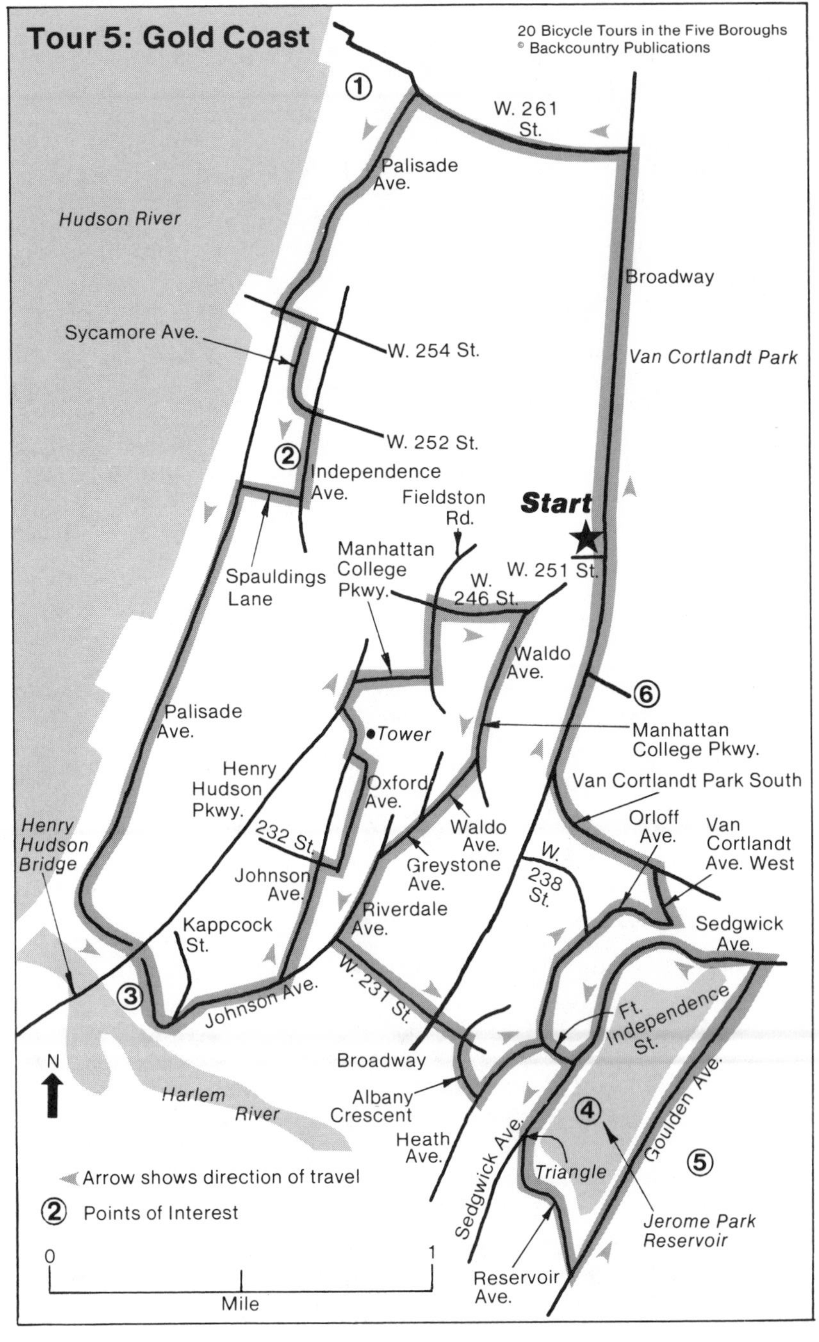

Tour 5: Gold Coast
20 Bicycle Tours in the Five Boroughs
© Backcountry Publications
W. 261 St.
Palisade Ave.
Hudson River
Broadway
Sycamore Ave.
W. 254 St.
Van Cortlandt Park
W. 252 St.
Independence Ave.
Fieldston Rd.
Start
Manhattan College Pkwy.
W. 251 St.
Spauldings Lane
W. 246 St.
Waldo Ave.
Palisade Ave.
Tower
Manhattan College Pkwy.
Henry Hudson Pkwy.
Oxford Ave.
Van Cortlandt Park South
Henry Hudson Bridge
232 St.
Waldo Ave.
Orloff Ave.
Van Cortlandt Ave. West
Greystone Ave.
Johnson Ave.
W. 238 St.
Riverdale Ave.
Kappcock St.
Sedgwick Ave.
Johnson Ave.
W. 231 St.
Ft. Independence St.
Broadway
Albany Crescent
Harlem River
Heath Ave.
Sedgwick Ave.
Goulden Ave.
Triangle
Jerome Park Reservoir
Reservoir Ave.
Arrow shows direction of travel
Points of Interest
0
1
Mile
N

nineteenth-century American Shakespearian actor Edwin Forrest. Forrest's eccentric home, Fonthill Castle, stands opposite the original red-brick college and now houses the campus library. For the best views of the campus, turn left into the campus, go past the attendant's booth, then proceed downhill around the castle. (1)

Leaving the campus, head south on Palisade Avenue (at the foot of 261st Street.

2.2 **Turn LEFT at West 254th Street, then take the first RIGHT at Sycamore Avenue.**

2.5 **Turn LEFT at the end, onto West 252nd Street, then make an immediate RIGHT at unmarked Independence Avenue, past Wave Hill on your right at West 249th Street.**

The Wave Hill Center for Environmental Studies occupies the grounds of an estate that was once home to Mark Twain, Theodore Roosevelt, and Arturo Toscanini, among others. The estate, a designated National Environmental Education Landmark, encompasses formal gardens, woods, huge old trees, and a nineteenth-century mansion. The center offers a variety of programs and field trips, including an outdoor sculpture show that runs from May through October. Open weekdays from 10:00 a.m. to 4:30 p.m., Saturday and Sunday from 10:00 a.m. to 5:30 p.m. Admission is free on weekdays. (2)

2.7 **Leaving Wave Hill, turn RIGHT onto Independence Avenue.**

2.8 **Independence Avenue curves sharply to the right and becomes unmarked West 248th Street (Spaulding Lane), which winds steeply downhill past the Riverdale Country School on your right.**

3.0 **At the bottom of the hill, Spaulding Lane curves sharply to the left and becomes Palisade Avenue at 247th Street. Continue STRAIGHT on Palisade Avenue for about a mile and a half.**

4.2 **Palisade Avenue curves to the left, downhill and underneath the Henry Hudson Bridge.**

The steeply sloped region at the confluence of the Harlem and Hudson rivers was named Spuyten Duyvil by the early Dutch settlers. Although the neighborhood has been overbuilt with enormous high-rise apartment buildings that hide the beauty of the cliffs, the sight of the elegant Henry Hudson Bridge spanning the gap between Spuyten Duyvil and Inwood Hill in Manhattan is still breathtaking. (3)

4.6 **Palisade Avenue becomes Johnson Avenue as you round a sharp curve to the left, past an apartment building on your right. Continue STRAIGHT, downhill on Johnson Avenue.**

Fonthill Castle.

5.0 Halfway down the hill, bear left at the first intersection to stay on Johnson Avenue, uphill again.

5.3 Turn RIGHT at West 232nd Street, then take an immediate LEFT at Oxford Avenue.

5.7 Turn RIGHT at the end of Oxford Avenue, onto Johnson Avenue, which merges into the service road of the Henry Hudson Parkway.

5.8 Bear LEFT around the stone tower at the next intersection, to stay on the Henry Hudson Parkway.

5.9 Then bear RIGHT at the next opportunity, onto unmarked Manhattan College Parkway.

6.1 Take the second LEFT at unmarked Fieldston Road, one block past Delafield Avenue.

6.3 Turn RIGHT at West 246th Street.

6.5 Turn RIGHT at Waldo Avenue.

6.7 Waldo Avenue becomes Manhattan College Parkway at 244th Street, past the campus of Manhattan College on your left.

6.8 Just past the campus, continue STRAIGHT, back onto Waldo Avenue. Do not follow Manhattan College Parkway as it curves to the left.

7.1 Waldo Avenue merges into Greystone Avenue at West 236th Street.

7.2 Turn LEFT at the end (at a flashing red light) onto Riverdale Avenue, downhill along a stone wall.

7.5 Turn LEFT at the bottom of the hill, onto West 231st Street.

7.9 Turn RIGHT at Albany Crescent, one block past Broadway.

8.0 Turn LEFT at Heath Avenue.

8.3 Turn RIGHT at Fort Independence Avenue.

8.4 Turn RIGHT at the end of Fort Independence Avenue, onto Sedgwick Avenue.

8.5 Take the first LEFT at Reservoir Avenue, along the Jerome Park Reservoir.

Originally part of the Old Croton Aqueduct water supply system, the reservoir (and nearby Jerome Avenue) takes its name from the Jerome Park Racetrack that occupied this site from 1876 to 1890. (4)

9.0 Turn LEFT at Goulden Avenue, continuing along the reservoir, past Lehman College on your right.

This campus of the City University of New York is best known for its Performing Arts Center, the first major cultural and entertainment center constructed in the Bronx. Legendary performers such as Itzhak Perlman, Marcel Marceau, and Dizzy Gillespie have appeared at this ultramodern center, which consists of a concert hall, two theaters, and a recital hall. (5)

9.9 Turn LEFT at Sedgwick Avenue, continuing around the reservoir.

10.7 Turn RIGHT at Fort Independence Avenue (one block past Giles), which curves to the right, downhill.

11.0 Bear RIGHT at West 238th Street, onto Orloff Avenue, uphill.

11.4 Turn LEFT at Van Cortlandt Avenue West. Van Cortlandt Avenue West becomes Van Cortlandt Park South.

11.8 Turn RIGHT at Broadway.

12.2 Turn RIGHT opposite no. 6035 Broadway into Van Cortlandt Park to visit the Van Cortlandt Manor, just inside the park.

George Washington slept here. Built in 1748 by the wealthy and influential Van Cortlandt family, this Georgian manor house served as headquarters for both American and British troops during the Revolution. The simple fieldstone exterior hides a lavishly decorated interior, furnished with many articles that belonged to the Van Cortlandts. To the north, overlooking the mansion, is Vault Hill, the family burial ground. There, in 1776, during the Revolutionary War, New York City's records were hidden while the British occupied the city. Open Tuesday through Saturday from 10:00 a.m. to 5:00 p.m., Sunday from 1:00 p.m. to 5:00 p.m. Admission is $1.00. (6)

Leaving the mansion, turn RIGHT onto Broadway, back to the starting point at West 251st Street.

Bicycle Shops

Sid's Bike Shop, 215 West 230th Street (at the corner of Broadway), Riverdale (212-549-8247)

Yonkers Bicycle Discount Center, 579 South Broadway (at the city line), Yonkers (914-963-4675)

View of the Hudson River from Wave Hill, Riverdale.

6

City Limits

Distance: 15 miles
Terrain: rolling
Traffic: moderate

What do Herman Melville, F. W. Woolworth, and Duke Ellington have in common? They're all buried in the northern Bronx, just below the Westchester County line, in the city's most illustrious burial ground. Beautiful Woodlawn Cemetery is the centerpiece of this tour through the northernmost reaches of the Bronx; it take you from the flatlands near Co-op City to the rolling hills along the city line just east of Van Cortlandt Park. As a matter of fact, this route goes beyond the New York City limits for about half a mile into the town of Yonkers before sweeping down again along the edge of Van Cortlandt Park and around Woodlawn. Because they are so far north, some of the communities in the area have an "upstate" flavor about them. The region is home to another of the borough's distinguished historic sites, the Valentine-Varian House, which houses the Museum of Bronx History.

Portions of the tour straddle one of the three north-south ridges that give the middle and western sections of the Bronx a rolling terrain, so be prepared for some minor elevations along the route. None of the hills are steep, but they won't go unnoticed by the unconditioned cyclist, either. The ride begins at Pelham Parkway and Eastchester Road. Drivers, take the Bruckner Expressway or the Hutchinson River Parkway to Pelham Parkway, then head west for about a mile to Eastchester Road.

Directions

0.0 Head north on Eastchester Road.

1.6 Turn RIGHT at Needham Avenue.

1.7 Turn LEFT at the end, onto East 222nd Street, then take an immediate RIGHT at Schieffelin Avenue.

2.2 Turn LEFT at the end, onto Baychester Avenue.

3.3 Baychester Avenue curves to the left around a railroad yard and becomes East 241st Street.

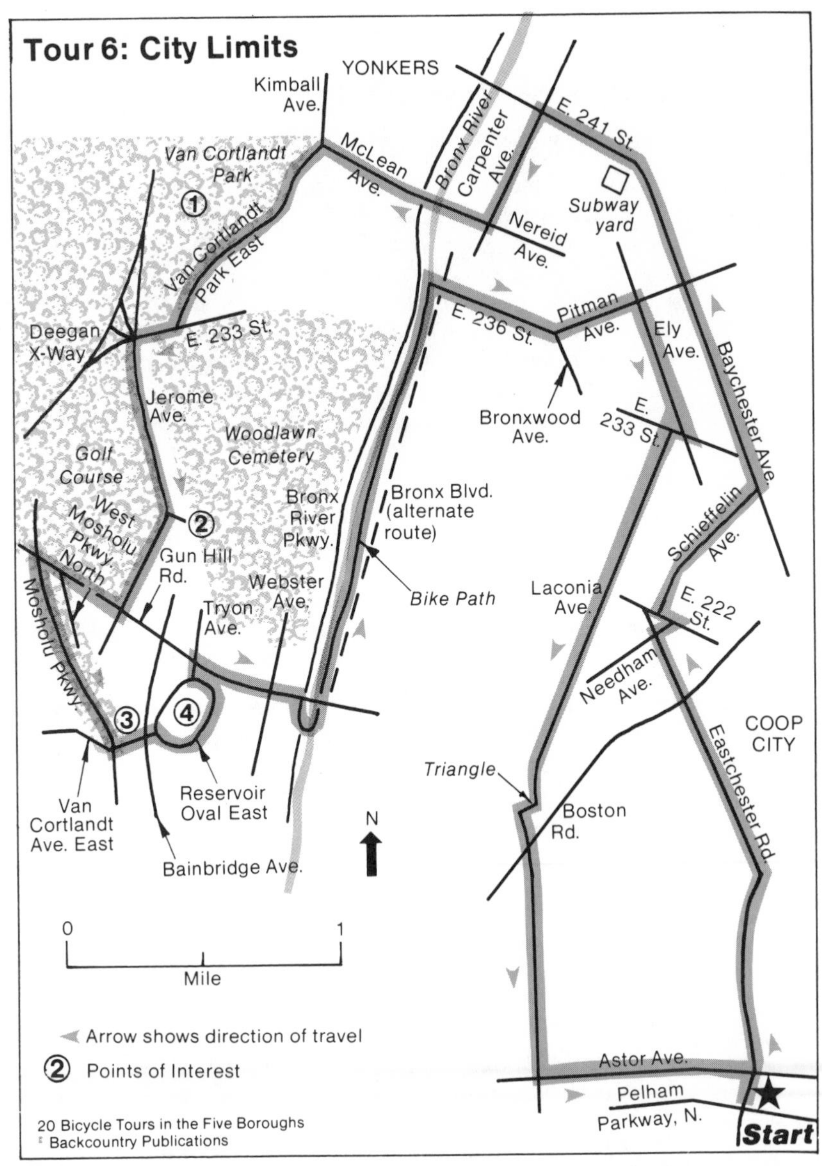

3.7 Turn LEFT at Carpenter Avenue, just *before* the bridge to Yonkers.

4.1 Turn RIGHT at Nereid Avenue, which becomes East 238th Street and takes you over another bridge into Yonkers.

As you cross the bridge, you are crossing the Bronx River. At this point it forms the boundary between New York City and Westchester County.

Coming off the bridge, continue STRAIGHT on McLean Avenue.

4.8 Turn LEFT at Kimball Avenue, at a busy intersection.

5.0 Kimball Avenue becomes Van Cortlandt Park East as you re-enter New York City at the corner of Van Cortlandt Park.

Van Cortlandt Park, on your right, is one of the largest and most varied of New York City's parks. Its facilities include golf courses, skating rinks, tennis courts, baseball fields, ski and hiking trails, bridle paths, and a thirty-six-acre lake. These amenities do not detract from the park's wilderness: there are wildlife and bird sanctuaries in the central and northern reaches of the huge tract. Unfortunately for cyclists, there is no continuous bicycle path inside the park, so pedalers must be content to cycle around the park's perimeter. (1)

5.6 Turn RIGHT at the end of Van Cortlandt Park East, onto East 233rd Street.

5.8 Take the first LEFT, at Jerome Avenue.

Be very careful at this confusing intersection. As you make the turn, you are facing an exit ramp of the Major Deegan Expressway.

6.3 Just before you reach the entrance to the Mosholu Golf Course on your right, turn LEFT into the main entrance of Woodlawn Cemetery.

The unspoiled tract of Woodlawn Cemetery is often overlooked, but it is one of the city's most unique sightseeing attractions. The burial ground is admired as much for its architectural wonders as for the caliber of the people who have been laid to rest there. F. W. Woolworth lies close to J. C. Penney. The meat-packing Armour family lies in a mausoleum of pinkish stone described in the *New York Times* as "vaguely reminiscent of ham," and so on. Woodlawn is a hall of fame of the most blue-blooded of high-society New Yorkers including six former mayors. Many of the crypts and tombstones carry interesting bits of trivia about their inhabitants. The grounds are also appreciated as a bird and tree sanctuary. Visitors must register with the attendant in the booth just inside the Jerome Avenue entrance. Admission is free. (2)

Leaving Woodlawn Cemetery, turn LEFT onto Jerome Avenue and continue STRAIGHT underneath the elevated subway line.

6.8 Turn RIGHT at Gun Hill Road.

7.1 Turn LEFT at Mosholu Parkway—*not* Mosholu Parkway North, which comes first. You should be going downhill and underneath a stone arch.

A famous grave in Woodlawn Cemetery.

.7 Turn LEFT at Van Cortlandt Avenue East.

.9 Turn LEFT at Bainbridge Avenue to visit the Museum of Bronx History on the northeast corner.

The rustic fieldstone farmhouse on the corner was built in 1758 by a blacksmith named Isaac Valentine. The Valentine-Varian House now houses the Museum of Bronx History and a fascinating research library run by the Bronx County Historical Society. On permanent display in the museum are such artifacts as 1923 box seats from Yankee Stadium and empty bottles and wooden taps from the breweries that were once in the area. The library downstairs contains loads of printed material, including old telephone directories, postcards, pamphlets, maps, and photographs related to the borough's history. The house was occupied from 1839 to 1841 by Isaac Varian, who was mayor of New York City at the time. The museum is open Saturday from 10:00 a.m. to 4:00 p.m. and Sunday from 1:00 p.m. to 5:00 p.m. Access to the library is by appointment only. (3)

Leaving the Valentine-Varian House, turn LEFT onto Bainbridge Avenue. Then take an immediate LEFT at Reservoir Oval East. Bear RIGHT around the Williamsbridge Oval.

Here behind the historic Valentine-Varian House is an interesting space. The Williamsbridge (or Reservoir) Oval, a circular embankment, encloses an elaborate city playground. Between 1888 and 1923, the embankment formed a dam to contain the waters of the Williamsbridge Reservoir, part of the city's water supply system. After the reservoir was abandoned, tunnels were cut through the embankment and the playground was installed. About halfway around the oval, at Putnam Place, is a dilapidated stone cottage that was formerly a "keeper's house," built in 1890 as part of the water supply system. (4)

8.5 **Turn RIGHT at Tryon Avenue, one block past Putnam Place. Take the first RIGHT at Gun Hill Road, going downhill.**

8.9 **At the bottom of the hill, cross Webster Avenue, then the southbound service road of the Bronx River Parkway.**

9.0 **Just *past* the *north*bound service road, turn RIGHT onto a bicycle path, which takes you downhill to the banks of the Bronx River.**

9.1 **At the bottom of this little hill, turn LEFT—or northbound—underneath an overpass and along the river. Continue north on the bicycle path along the Bronx River.**

For a smoother ride you can cycle along Bronx Boulevard, the street that parallels the bike route.

10.5 **Turn RIGHT at East 236th Street, going uphill.**

10.9 **East 236th Street curves to the left and becomes Pitman Avenue as you cross Bronxwood Avenue.**

11.2 **Turn RIGHT at Ely Avenue.**

11.6 **Turn RIGHT at East 233rd Street. Then take an immediate LEFT at Laconia Avenue.**

13.0 **At Boston Road you must go around a little triangle to continue on Laconia Avenue.**

13.8 **Turn LEFT at Astor Avenue.**

14.5 **Turn RIGHT at Eastchester Road, which leads you back to the starting point at Pelham Parkway.**

Bicycle Shops

Arrow Cycle Service, 4053 White Plains Road (near East 228th Street), Williamsbridge (212-547-2656)

Bronx Bike Center, 912 East Gun Hill Road (near White Plains Road) (212-798-3242)

County Cycle Center, 941 McLean Avenue, Yonkers (914-237-8641)

7
The "Other" Bronx

Distance: 23 miles
Terrain: flat
Traffic: light

A pleasant surprise awaits those with preconceived notions of the Bronx as an urban wasteland filled with decaying high-rises and rubble-strewn lots. This tour of the east Bronx takes in some of the most scenic and desirable territory in the entire city. Tucked between the graceful spans of the Whitestone and Throgs Neck bridges is the sleepy waterside community of Throgs Neck, where no home is more than a few blocks away from a bay, creek, inlet, or river. A little farther along the route is mile-long City Island, where you can sample some of the best seafood in the country and see the boatyards that gave this island its reputation as a world-class yacht-building center. In between these two unexpected localities lies one of the city's most unspoiled recreation areas, Pelham Bay Park, with over two thousand acres of woodlands, tidal estuaries, and salt marshes, and a smooth white crescent beach fronting on the waters of Long Island Sound. Long stretches of carefree cycling, away from the borough's major traffic arteries, make this area a pedaler's delight.

The trip begins at the parking field in Ferry Point Park, located at the foot of the Whitestone Bridge in the Throgs Neck section of the Bronx. To get there, take the Hutchinson River Parkway's southbound service road and bear right just before reaching the toll plaza.

Directions

0.0 **Leaving the parking field in Ferry Point Park, turn LEFT onto the park road, which will take you underneath the Whitestone Bridge and onto the northbound service road of the Hutchinson River Parkway.**

1.2 **Turn RIGHT at the traffic light, onto Lafayette Avenue.**

1.9 **Turn RIGHT at East Tremont Avenue.**

3.1 **Turn LEFT at the end, onto Schurz Avenue.**

3.4 **Turn RIGHT at Pennyfield Avenue.**

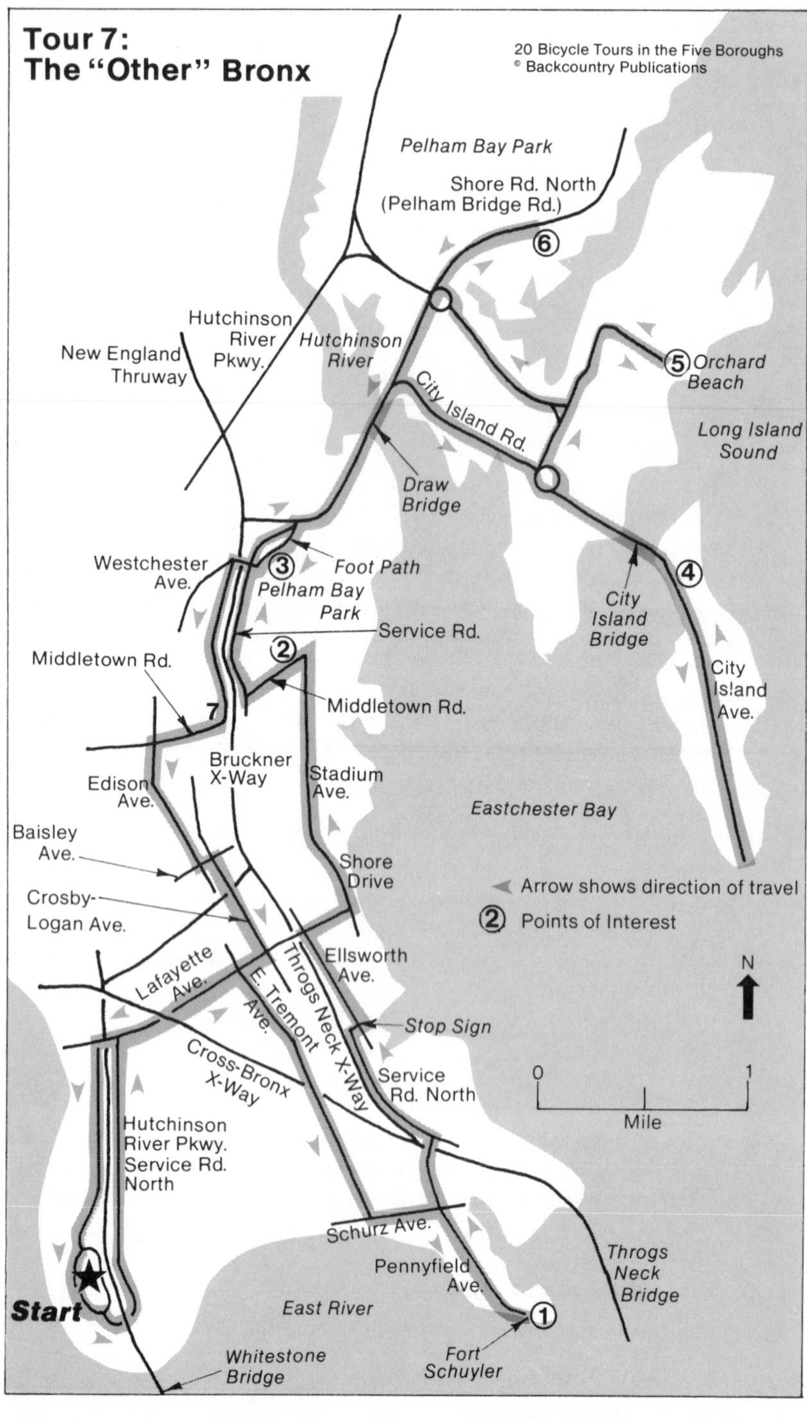
Tour 7:
The "Other" Bronx
20 Bicycle Tours in the Five Boroughs
© Backcountry Publications
Pelham Bay Park
Shore Rd. North
(Pelham Bridge Rd.)
6
Hutchinson River Pkwy.
Hutchinson River
New England Thruway
5 Orchard Beach
City Island Rd.
Long Island Sound
Draw Bridge
Westchester Ave.
3
Foot Path
Pelham Bay Park
4
City Island Bridge
Service Rd.
2
Middletown Rd.
Middletown Rd.
7
City Island Ave.
Bruckner X-Way
Edison Ave.
Stadium Ave.
Eastchester Bay
Baisley Ave.
Shore Drive
Arrow shows direction of travel
Crosby-Logan Ave.
2 Points of Interest
Lafayette Ave.
E. Tremont Ave.
Throgs Neck X-Way
Ellsworth Ave.
N
Stop Sign
Cross-Bronx X-Way
Service Rd. North
0
1
Mile
Hutchinson River Pkwy. Service Rd. North
Schurz Ave.
Pennyfield Ave.
Throgs Neck Bridge
Start
East River
1
Fort Schuyler
Whitestone Bridge

4.0 Turn LEFT into the circular entrance to the State University of New York Maritime College and Fort Schuyler.

A ride along the perimeter road will take you past the modern buildings of the college and into the stone fortifications of this landmark site, built in the 1830s as one of a series of forts to protect the approaches to New York Harbor. You may be required to register with the guard at the entrance. Afterward, you're free to wander the grounds and visit the interior courts. At the tip of the promontory you can see Fort Totten, across Long Island Sound in Queens. The two strongholds were designed to attack any enemy approaching the Port of New York via Long Island Sound with cannon fire. Today, much of the fort has been adapted for classroom use by the college. You may glimpse the S.S. *Empire State,* a former Navy flagship that is now used as the college's training ship. It is docked beneath the Throg's Neck Bridge. (1)

5.7 Leaving Fort Schuyler via the main entrance, turn RIGHT onto Pennyfield Avenue.

6.6 Turn LEFT at the northbound service road of the Throgs Neck Expressway.

7.3 Turn LEFT at a stop sign at the end of the service road, onto Ellsworth Avenue.

7.7 Turn RIGHT at Lafayette Avenue.

7.9 Turn LEFT at the end, onto Shore Drive, which becomes Stadium Avenue.

9.0 Turn LEFT at the end, onto Middletown Road, past Rice Memorial Stadium on your right.

This concrete stadium is noted for the small replica of a Greek temple set atop the bleachers. It frames a statue by Louis St. Lannes, "The American Boy" (visible from inside the park). The stadium itself was donated in 1916 by the widow of Isaac L. Rice, whose name is associated with developments in electric storage batteries. In honor of the Rices, nearby streets were named after units of electrical measurement: Watt Street, Ampere Street, Ohm Street, and so on. (2)

9.4 Turn RIGHT, at the end of Middletown Road, onto the service road of the Bruckner Expressway.

10.0 Bear RIGHT past Westchester Avenue, following signs to City Island.

The Pelham Bay Park World War Memorial, on your right just past Westchester Avenue, is considered one of the handsomest and best-maintained monuments in the city. It was sculpted by Belle Kinney in 1925. (3)

North Wind Undersea Institute on City Island.

11.0 Cross the Hutchinson River Drawbridge, and turn RIGHT at the first traffic light onto City Island Road, following signs to City Island.

11.7 Go around the traffic circle, following signs to City Island.

12.4 Cross the City Island Bridge, then continue STRAIGHT on City Island Avenue.

City Island was originally part of Westchester County. In 1895, its citizens voted to "secede" and become part of the Bronx, in return for a new school and bridge. The island has a long history as a world-class yacht-building center which has turned out several America's Cup defenders.

City Island is also home to the recently opened North Wind Undersea Institute, an environmental organization dedicated to ocean research and whale rescue. The North Wind Museum, at 610 City Island Avenue, near the foot of the bridge, houses a fascinating exhibit of historic whaling artifacts, deepsea diving gear, sunken treasure artifacts and uncommonly beautiful seashells. But the museum's most popular attraction is undoubtedly the three harbor seals, members of the Seal Search and Recovery Team, being trained to bring emergency air and tools to divers working underwater. You may be lucky enough to observe one of the daily training sessions. The museum is open 7 days year round, from 10:00 a.m. to 5:00 p.m. Admission is $3.50 for adults. (4)

Leaving the North Wind Museum, turn LEFT onto City Island Avenue and continue STRAIGHT to the tip of the island, if desired, then retrace your path back to the City Island Bridge.

14.1 Leaving City Island, cross the bridge.

14.7 At the first traffic circle, turn RIGHT, following signs to Orchard Beach.

15.2 Turn RIGHT at the next traffic circle, into Orchard Beach.

No visit to City Island is complete without a visit to her neighbor—clean, white Orchard Beach on Long Island Sound. Even if it's not swimming season, a walk along the beach is memorable for the view of the sound and to see the functional design of the WPA-built bathhouses. (5)

Leaving Orchard Beach, turn LEFT at the traffic circle, then bear RIGHT, following signs to the Hutchinson River Parkway.

16.8 Bear RIGHT at the next traffic circle, following signs to Shore Road North.

About half a mile down Shore Road North, on your right, is a stone gate that marks the entrance to the elegant Bartow-Pell Mansion. Built around 1836 by the descendants of a wealthy colonial family, it was restored and furnished with museum pieces in 1914 by the International Garden Club. The manor is most admired for its sunken garden, which extends toward Long Island Sound from the rear of the building. Open Tuesday, Friday, and Sunday from 2:00 p.m. to 4:00 p.m. Admission is $1.00. (6)

Leaving the Bartow-Pell Mansion, turn LEFT onto Shore Road North. Continue STRAIGHT past the next traffic circle and over the drawbridge.

18.3 When you come to a fork in the road and a sign indicating the New England Thruway, cross Shore Road and pick up the footpath along

the edge of Pelham Bay Park, facing traffic. *Do not* go toward the New England Thruway. Continue along the footpath.

18.5 Turn RIGHT at Westchester Avenue, then take the first LEFT onto the southbound service road of the Bruckner Expressway.

19.1 Turn RIGHT at Middletown Road.

On the southwest corner of the Bruckner Expressway and Middletown Road, behind a barbed-wire fence, are the grounds of the Heye Annex of the Museum of the American Indian. You can't go inside this warehouse and research center, but you can peek through the fence at the display of totem poles and wigwams on the lawn. (7)

19.5 Turn LEFT at Edison Avenue.

20.1 Turn LEFT at Baisley Avenue.

20.2 Turn RIGHT at Crosby Avenue, which becomes Logan Avenue.

20.6 Turn RIGHT at Lafayette Avenue.

21.5 Turn LEFT at the southbound service road of the Hutchinson River Parkway (*not* the Cross Bronx Expressway), back to the parking field in Ferry Point Park.

Bicycle Shops

Westchester Bicycle Pro Shop, 2611 Westchester Avenue (212-409-1114)
Tremont Cycle Center, 3635 East Tremont Avenue (near Randall Avenue), Throgs Neck (212-823-1098)

Fort Schuyler, Throgs Neck.

8

Queens "North Shore" Tour

Distance: 21 miles
Terrain: rolling
Traffic: moderate

Say "north shore" to most New Yorkers, and they'll probably think of rambling estates overlooking Long Island Sound in places like Oyster Bay and Glen Cove. But geographically speaking, Long Island's North Shore begins in Queens, well within New York City limits; and the communities along Queens's North Shore have a flavor all their own that is somewhere between that of Nassau County to the east and that of the metropolitan area to the west.

This tour takes in several Queens shoreline neighborhoods. All have a suburban quality yet are definitely within the New York City tradition of blending the old with the new. At the western edge of the route, College Point calls to mind a nineteenth-century factory town, with its shingled houses crowded close together on narrow streets. Traveling eastward, long stretches of trim houses and well-kept lawns evoke modern-day suburbia. And finally, the easternmost portion of the ride at Douglaston and Little Neck shows the influence of that other North Shore—the one with the estates. Gracious homes set on broad lawns overlooking Little Neck Bay present a genteel, resortlike aspect like that of neighboring Nassau County.

Begin at the Pathmark shopping center on the south side of the Whitestone Expressway at Linden Place in Flushing. To get there, take the Whitestone Expressway (678) to Exit 14 (Linden Place) and look for the shopping center off the eastbound service road of the expressway.

Directions

0.0 **Leaving the shopping center parking lot, turn RIGHT onto the eastbound service road of the Whitestone Expressway, then make a U-TURN at the traffic light, onto the westbound service road.**

0.5 **Turn RIGHT at the end, onto College Point Boulevard.**

1.7 **Turn LEFT at 23rd Avenue.**

1.8 **Turn RIGHT at 120th Street.**

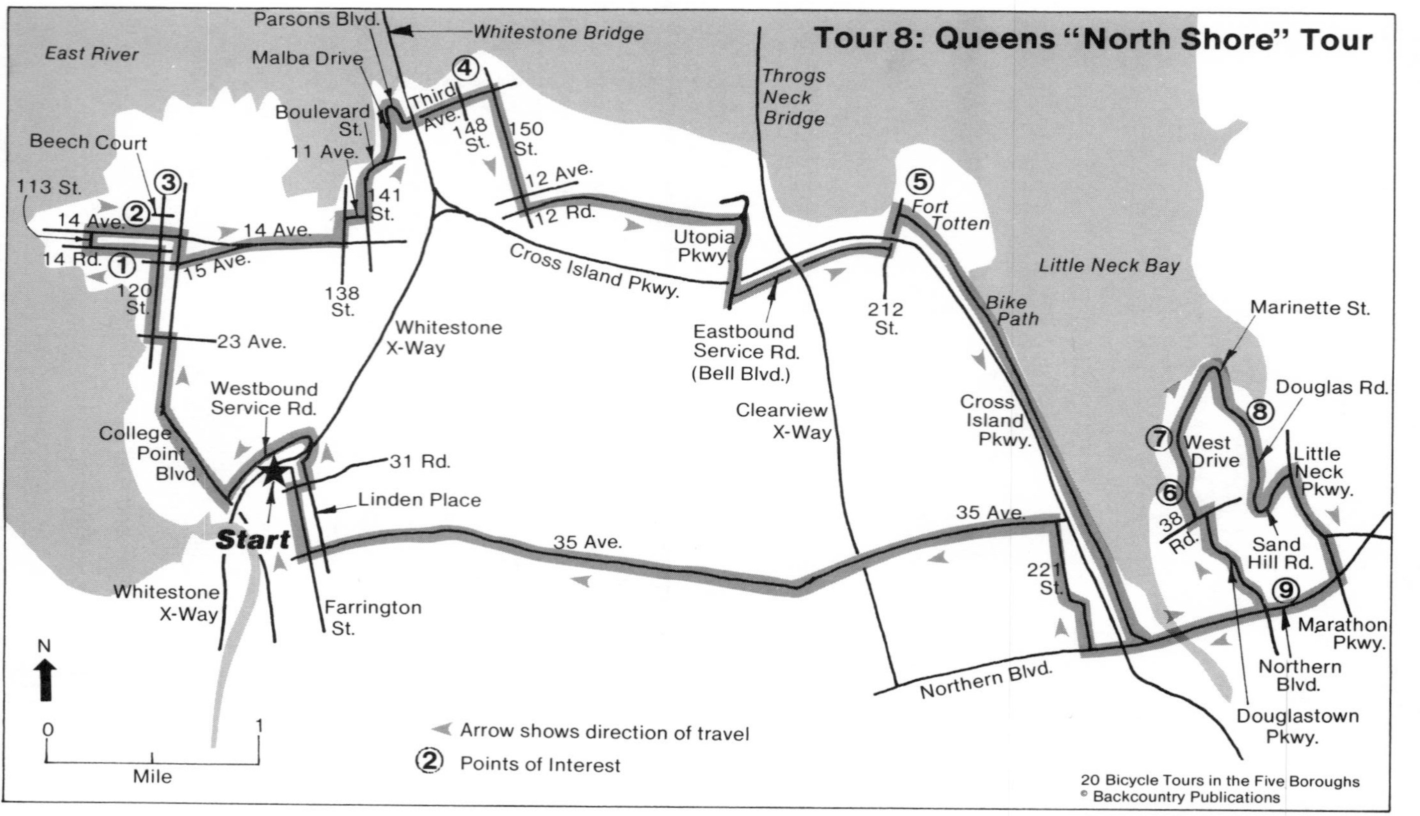
Tour 8: Queens "North Shore" Tour
East River
Parsons Blvd.
Whitestone Bridge
Malba Drive
Boulevard St.
Beech Court
11 Ave.
113 St.
14 Ave.
14 Rd.
14 Ave.
15 Ave.
120 St.
141 St.
138 St.
23 Ave.
Third Ave.
148 St.
150 St.
12 Ave.
12 Rd.
Cross Island Pkwy.
Whitestone X-Way
Throgs Neck Bridge
Utopia Pkwy.
Eastbound Service Rd. (Bell Blvd.)
Clearview X-Way
Fort Totten
212 St.
Bike Path
Little Neck Bay
Cross Island Pkwy.
Marinette St.
Douglas Rd.
West Drive
Little Neck Pkwy.
38 Rd.
Sand Hill Rd.
Marathon Pkwy.
Northern Blvd.
Douglastown Pkwy.
35 Ave.
35 Ave.
221 St.
Northern Blvd.
Westbound Service Rd.
College Point Blvd.
31 Rd.
Linden Place
Start
Whitestone X-Way
Farrington St.
N
0
1
Mile
Arrow shows direction of travel
Points of Interest
20 Bicycle Tours in the Five Boroughs
© Backcountry Publications

2.3 Turn LEFT at 14th *Road.* (not 14th Avenue)

College Point had its origins during the early industrial period of the United States, when many former agricultural communities grew into "mill towns," each with its factory and rows of company housing. College Point has somehow retained its small-town atmosphere in the midst of the city's most rapidly growing borough.

On your left at 115th Street (and 14th Road) is a 115-year-old landmark building, the Poppenhusen Institute, which housed the first free kindergarten in the United States. Conrad Poppenhusen, the German-born industrialist who founded and operated the factories around which the community developed, built the Institute to provide education for his workers and their families. The building is an example of the civic architecture of the post–Civil War period. (1)

2.6 Turn RIGHT at 113th Street.

3.0 Turn RIGHT at 14th Avenue.

The First Reformed Church and Sunday School of College Point, on your left at 118th Street, is a well-preserved example of the rural architecture characteristic of many Queens communities during the late 1800s. (2)

Two blocks past the church, detour left into Beech Court and circle around a cozy little enclave of large and comfortable houses surrounding a common green. (3) Return to 14th Avenue.

3.4 Turn RIGHT at College Point Boulevard. Take the second LEFT at 15th Avenue, which merges into 14th Avenue.

The next mile will take you over a hazardous stretch of very bad road, with no shoulder and heavy traffic. Pedal carefully; conditions will soon improve.

4.2 Turn LEFT at 138th Street.

4.4 Turn RIGHT at the end, onto unmarked 11th Avenue.

4.6 Turn LEFT at 141st Street. 141st Street curves to the right and becomes Boulevard at the waterfront.

4.8 Bear LEFT at the first opportunity, onto Malba Drive. Malba Drive curves to the right and becomes Parsons Boulevard near the foot of the Whitestone Bridge.

5.2 Take the first LEFT at Third Avenue, underneath the bridge.

Whitestone looks like any other Queens bedroom community. But the neighborhood includes a number of historic houses. Number 2-11 147th Street, to your left off Third Avenue, is a restored pre-Revolutionary building that was originally part of a huge estate. The property is surrounded by a high wooden fence. For a better view, make this little detour: Proceed along Third Avenue, turn left at

148th Street, then keep bearing left into a cul-de-sac, at the end of which the house can be seen through the bushes on your left. (4)

Continue STRAIGHT, on Third Avenue.

5.7 **Turn RIGHT at 150th Street.**

6.2 **Turn LEFT at 12th *Road* (not 12th Avenue).**

7.2 **Turn RIGHT at the end, onto Utopia Parkway, which curves right, then left.**

7.6 **Turn LEFT at the traffic light, onto the eastbound service road (Bell Boulevard) of the Cross Island Parkway.**

8.3 **Turn LEFT at 212th Street, underneath the highway, then RIGHT onto the bicycle path (also open to traffic) that runs alongside the Cross Island Parkway, facing traffic.**

Old Fort Totten, at the end of 212th Street, is a historic site. Designed by Robert E. Lee, it was built in 1857 as the companion fort to Fort Schuyler, across the bay in the Bronx. Entrance to the fort is by special permission of the U.S. Army. (5)

Continue east along the bikeway. Little Neck Bay is on your left.

11.0 **Turn LEFT at the end of the bikeway, onto busy Northern Boulevard.**

11.5 **Take your first LEFT at Douglaston Parkway.**

12.1 **Turn LEFT at 38th Road, onto West Drive.**

Number 126 West Drive, at Alston Place opposite Ridge Road, is a landmark eighteenth-century Dutch colonial farmhouse with hand-hewn shingles and "salt-box" roof, one of only a few such houses to remain in New York City. A little farther down the road, at 600 West Drive, is the Douglaston Clubhouse, the former mansion of a wealthy colonial family. (6, 7)

13.0 **Turn RIGHT at the end of West Drive, onto Marinette Street, which becomes Douglas Road.**

13.7 **Turn LEFT at Sand Hill Road, downhill into Udall's Cove.**

A group of conservationists banded together and managed to preserve this area of natural wetlands and marshes, in an environment where suburban sprawl is rampant. (8)

13.9 **Turn RIGHT at the stop sign, crossing the railroad tracks, onto Little Neck Parkway.**

14.2 **Bear RIGHT at the first traffic light, onto Marathon Parkway.**

14.4 **Turn RIGHT at Northern Boulevard.**

On your right at 244th Street is Little Neck's most historic site, Zion Church. Surrounding the graceful white building is a tiny cemetery

The bicycle path along Little Neck Bay.

where several Matinecoc Indians are buried along with former illustrious citizens of the community. The grounds are open to the public. (9)

Continue west on Northern Boulevard, pedaling carefully on this busy, hazardous stretch, which includes several highway access ramps.

15.8 **Turn RIGHT at 221st Street.**

16.5 **Turn LEFT at the end, onto 35th Avenue.**

17.8 **At Francis Lewis Boulevard bear RIGHT to stay on 35th Avenue.**

20.5 **Turn RIGHT at Farrington Street, which will take you back to the Pathmark shopping center, on your left at 31st Road.**

Bicycle Shops

Century Bicycle Shop, 14–18 150th Street (near Cross Island Parkway), Whitestone (718–767–2772)

North Shore Cyclery, 3 Northern Boulevard (at the city line), Great Neck (516–482–1193)

9
Queens Heritage Trail

Distance: 15 miles
Terrain: rolling
Traffic: light

A cluster of historic buildings near downtown Flushing has been dubbed the Flushing Freedom Mile by local historical societies. Among these landmarks—most of them legacies of the community's Quaker heritage—are the two oldest private houses in Queens, a Quaker meeting house, and a magnificent Weeping Beech Tree planted in 1847 that is now recognized as New York's only "living" landmark. As a matter of fact, Flushing has long been noted for the beauty and variety of its trees, most of which are remnants of the community's nineteenth-century heyday as the horticultural center of America. In homage to her colonial past *and* her botanical prominence, neighborhood streets are named after local heroes (Bowne, Parsons, Barclay) or after trees (dozens of species are represented, from Maple to Magnolia). And one of the borough's longest thoroughfares, nearby Francis Lewis Boulevard, bears the name of the only signer of the Declaration of Independence who resided in Queens County.

The Flushing Historic District is the centerpiece of this tour, but the ride also takes in a string of handsome suburban-style communities and broad leafy parks and playgrounds stretching to the east and south. Cycling in the area is a relaxing experience, mostly on lightly traveled roads—with the exception of Northern Boulevard near downtown Flushing, which is a *very* busy commercial district. The route begins at Francis Lewis Boulevard (exit 26) and the Long Island Expressway, at the edge of Cunningham Park. There is a Waldbaum's shopping center with a large parking lot just off the westbound service road of the expressway.

Directions

0.0 Leaving the Waldbaum's parking lot, head south on Francis Lewis Boulevard, crossing the Long Island Expressway.

The woods on either side of the boulevard belong to Cunningham Park, six hundred forested acres with nature trails, picnic areas, ballfields, and playgrounds, and with outdoor concerts and theater in the summer. (1)

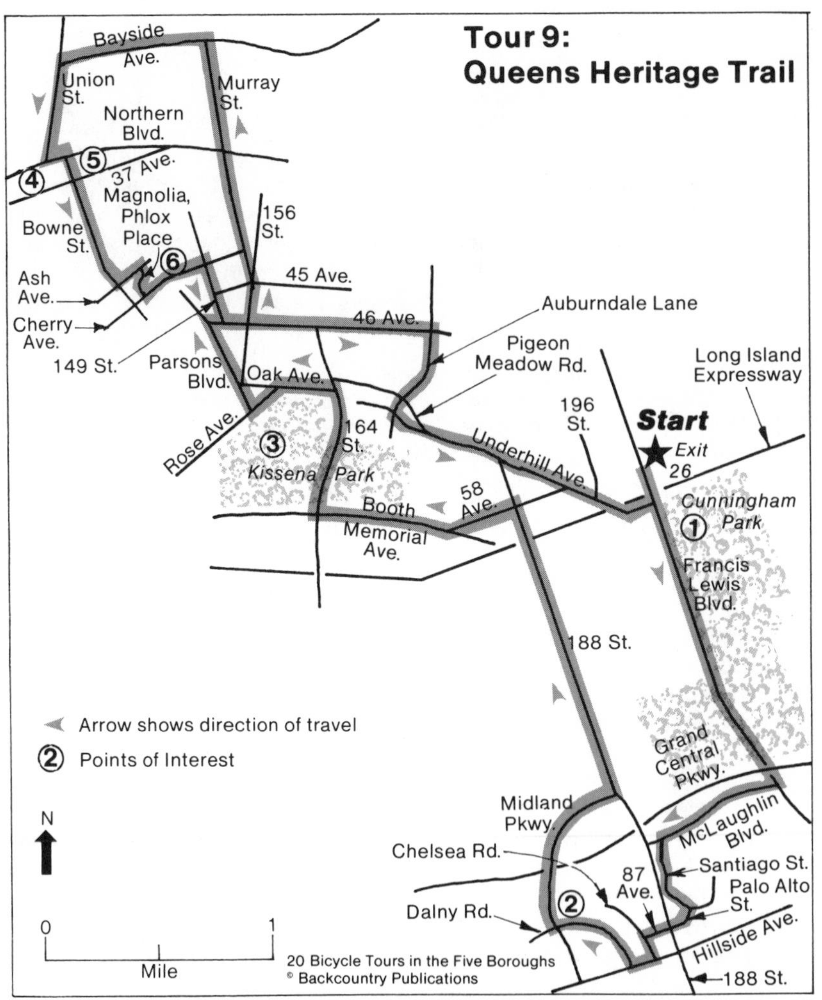

1.4 Turn RIGHT at McLaughlin Avenue, just past the Grand Central Parkway.

2.0 Turn LEFT at Santiago Street. The street sign is hidden by foliage in the summer. It is one block past Palo Alto Street.

2.3 Turn RIGHT at the end, onto Palo Alto Street, which becomes 87th Road as you cross 188th Street.

2.5 Turn LEFT at the end, onto Chelsea Street.

2.6 Turn RIGHT at Hillside Avenue.

2.7 Take the first RIGHT at Dalny Road.

3.1 Turn RIGHT at Midland Parkway.

This is the community of Jamaica Estates. The canopy of towering oaks shading Midland Parkway and its islands is the hallmark of this well-heeled neighborhood, which ranks alongside Forest Hills as a well-established pocket of prosperity in the borough. The Tudor mansions along its winding hilly roads, as well as the British street names (Aberdeen, Cambridge, Kent), reflect the locality's roots as a haven for wealthy British expatriates. Jamaica, incidentally, is named after the Jameco Indians, who originally occupied the land. (2)

3.9 Turn LEFT at the end, onto 188th Street.

5.2 Turn LEFT at 58th Avenue, which merges into Booth Memorial Avenue as you cross Utopia Parkway.

6.1 Turn RIGHT at 164th Street.

6.6 Turn LEFT at Oak Avenue.

6.9 Take the first LEFT, at Rose Avenue, along the edge of Kissena Park.

7.0 Turn LEFT at Parsons Boulevard, into the Kissena Park Historic Grove.

A grove of rare oriental trees was planted here by Samuel Bowne Parsons in the 1850s during Flushing's heyday as the horticultural center of America. This grove of exotic trees was rediscovered only in 1981. Much of the original nursery stock—over a hundred varieties—was left undisturbed when the land was bought by the city as a part of Kissena Park. The trees are marked with identifying plaques, and a guide to the grove is posted at the entrance. Walking tours are occasionally offered by the Urban Park Rangers. (718-699-4204) (3)

Leaving the grove, head up Parsons Boulevard.

7.5 Turn RIGHT at 46th Avenue.

7.6 Take the second LEFT at 156th Street.

7.8 Bear LEFT onto Murray Street as you cross 45th Avenue.

8.8 Turn LEFT at Bayside Avenue.

9.6 Turn LEFT at the end, onto Union Street.

10.0 Turn RIGHT at Northern Boulevard, and follow it for two blocks to the Quaker meeting house, on the south side of the boulevard, opposite Linden Place.

Quaker Meeting House in Flushing.

This landmark Quaker meeting house, built in 1694, is still in use today for religious activities by the Society of Friends. At the rear of the simple wooden building, facing a tiny graveyard, are two doors once used as separate entrances for men and women. The building is open to the public on the first and third Sundays of every month except August, from 2:00 p.m. to 4:00 p.m. (4)

Leaving the Quaker meeting house, turn RIGHT onto Northern Boulevard.

10.4 Take the second RIGHT, at Bowne Street.

10.5 Take the first LEFT, opposite 37th Avenue, onto Weeping Beech Park.

At 37-01 Bowne Street, next to Weeping Beech Park, stands the oldest dwelling in Queens, the Bowne House. It was built in 1661 by John Bowne and inhabited by nine successive generations of his family, until 1945. In the seventeenth century, the house was used for clandestine meetings of the outlawed Quaker sect, of which Bowne himself was a devout member. Two hundred years later, the house served as a stop on the Underground Railroad, which transported slaves to freedom before the Civil War. The house is filled with impeccably preserved furnishings, heirlooms and kitchen utensils. Open Tuesday, Thursday, Saturday, and Sunday from 2:30 p.m. to 4:30 p.m.

Now walk through the playground in Weeping Beech Park to 37th Avenue and Parsons Boulevard. Here stands another landmark dwelling, a Dutch colonial farmhouse built in 1774 by a Quaker farmer. The Kingsland House is used as headquarters for the Queens Historical Society, which maintains a library and changing exhibitions on Queens life and history.

In the backyard of the Kingsland House is the famous Weeping Beech Tree. It was planted in 1847 by nurseryman Samuel Parsons, a descendant of the Bowne family; he was also responsible for the Kissena Park Historic Grove. It is said that all other weeping beeches in the United States come from this tree. Today the tree is over sixty feet tall with a trunk circumference of fourteen feet. It is officially recognized as a "living" landmark. (5)

Leaving Weeping Beech Park, go back to Bowne Street and turn LEFT.

Historic Kingsland House and Weeping Beech Tree.

11.0 Turn LEFT at Ash Avenue.

Another unique Queens enclave, these turn-of-the-century houses are in varying stages of preservation, with old-fashioned porches, chimneys, towers, and mansards. They were saved from the wrecker's ball in the late 1920s when an apartment house was built in the area. (6)

11.1 Take the second RIGHT at Magnolia Place, which curves to the right and merges into Phlox Place.

11.2 Turn LEFT at the end of Phlox Place, onto Cherry Avenue.

11.7 Turn RIGHT at 149th Street.

11.8 Turn LEFT at the end, onto 46th Avenue.

12.7 Turn RIGHT at Auburndale Lane, which becomes Fresh Meadow Lane.

13.2 Turn LEFT at Underhill Avenue. The street sign may be hidden by foliage. It is one block past Pidgeon Meadow Road.

13.8 Turn RIGHT at 196th Street, onto a pedestrian overpass to cross the Long Island Expressway.

14.0 Turn RIGHT at the bottom of the ramp, onto the eastbound service road of the expressway.

14.3 Take the first LEFT at Francis Lewis Boulevard, back to the shopping center on the westbound service road.

Bicycle Shops

Bayside Bicycle, Inc., 214-20 73rd Avenue, Bayside (718-776-5161)
The Bicycle Place, 45-70 Kissena Boulevard, Flushing (718-358-0986)
Buddy's Schwinn Bicycles, 79-30 Parsons Boulevard, Flushing (718-591-9180)
Master Cycle, Inc., 159-01 Northern Boulevard, Flushing (718-445-9118)
Roberts Bicycle, 190-11 Union Turnpike, Flushing (718-468-2407)
Roberts Bayside Bicycle, 33-13 Francis Lewis Boulevard, Bayside (718-353-5432)

10
A Touch of Class

Distance: 13 miles
Terrain: flat
Traffic: light

Stretched between two busy highways near the heart of the city's largest borough is a broad expanse of well-manicured lawns and trees, sprinkled with the souvenirs of two World's Fairs. Flushing Meadow–Corona Park, with its own museum, zoo, theater, restaurant, lakes, meadows, and giant Unisphere, is Queens's most beloved attraction and a widely recognized symbol of the borough. Bordering this oasis to the southwest is a community of estatelike homes with trendy boutiques, a world-class tennis stadium, and a fanciful replica of an English Tudor village. Classy Forest Hills is among the city's most distinctive neighborhoods. This is an easy ride through two of the borough's most popular destinations, both of which are ideally suited for a visit on two wheels: Flushing Meadow Park is well supplied with a network of smooth, paved paths and roadways; and Forest Hills Gardens is a nearly traffic-free enclave of quiet, hidden lanes and byways. The tour should appeal, therefore, to the novice or unconditioned cyclist as well as to the experienced tourist looking to explore a most delightful pocket of the city.

There is one restriction: Since the route begins at Shea Stadium, home of the N.Y. Mets, you might want to avoid this tour on game days if you are driving to the site. On those days, traffic around the stadium is extremely heavy and it is difficult, if not impossible, to park in the vicinity. At other times, begin at the Shea Stadium parking field, at Roosevelt Avenue and 126th Street, in Corona, Queens.

Directions

0.0 Leaving the parking lot, turn LEFT onto 126th Street.

0.2 Turn LEFT at the traffic light, onto Northern Boulevard, then bear RIGHT, following signs to the Queens Museum.

0.4 Bear LEFT around the semicircle, following signs to Shea Stadium and the Queens Museum.

0.5 Turn RIGHT at the traffic circle facing the stadium, then bear LEFT so

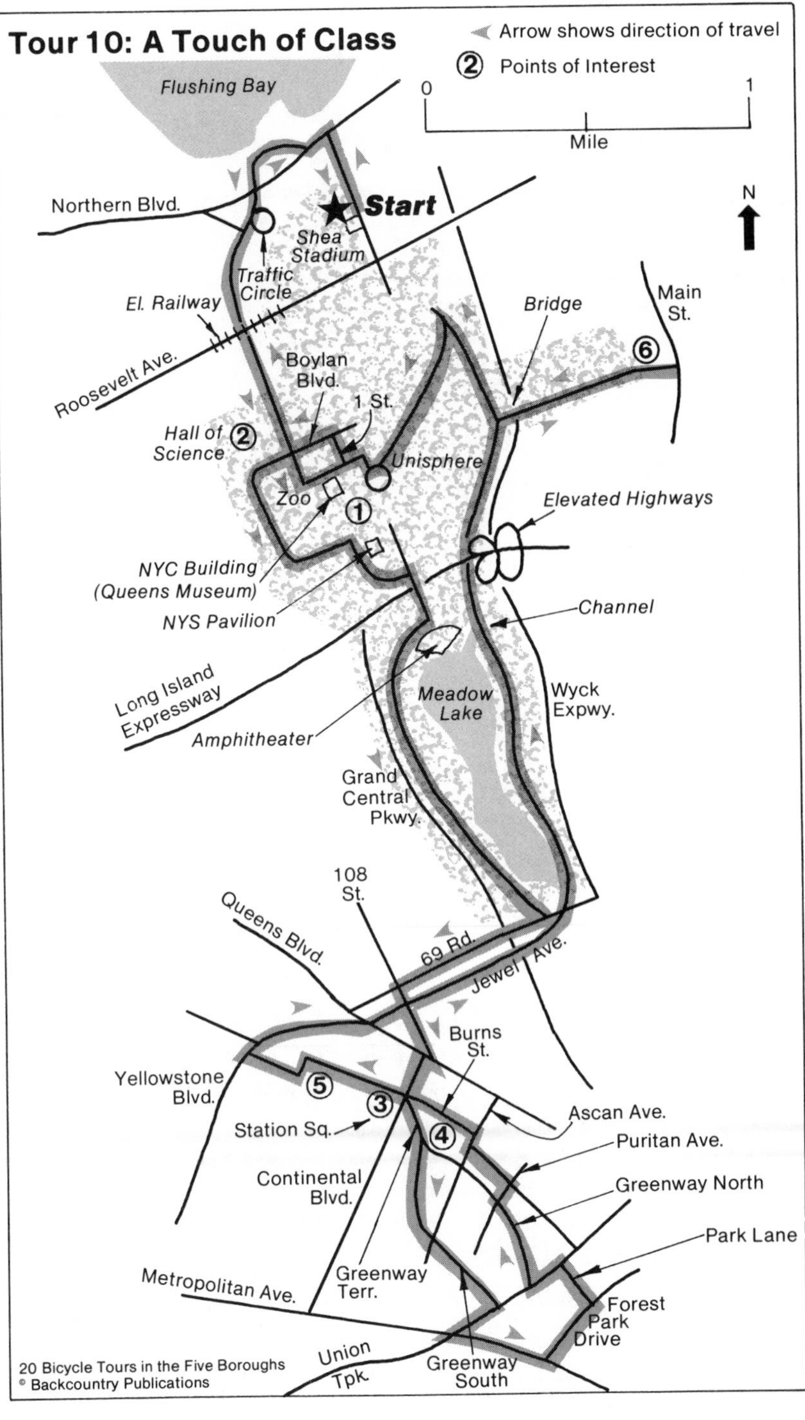
Tour 10: A Touch of Class
Arrow shows direction of travel
② Points of Interest
0
1
Mile
N
Flushing Bay
Northern Blvd.
Start
Shea Stadium
Traffic Circle
El. Railway
Roosevelt Ave.
Boylan Blvd.
1 St.
Hall of Science ②
Unisphere
Zoo
①
Main St.
Bridge
⑥
Elevated Highways
NYC Building (Queens Museum)
NYS Pavilion
Channel
Long Island Expressway
Meadow Lake
Wyck Expwy.
Amphitheater
Grand Central Pkwy.
108 St.
Queens Blvd.
69 Rd.
Jewel Ave.
Burns St.
Yellowstone Blvd.
⑤
③
Station Sq.
④
Ascan Ave.
Puritan Ave.
Greenway North
Continental Blvd.
Park Lane
Metropolitan Ave.
Greenway Terr.
Forest Park Drive
Union Tpk.
Greenway South
20 Bicycle Tours in the Five Boroughs
© Backcountry Publications

that you pass to the right of the stadium and underneath an elevated railway. Continue following signs to the Queens Museum.

1.5 Turn LEFT in front of the Queens Museum.

Flushing Meadow Park was the site of two World's Fairs, in 1939 and 1964. The New York City Building, in which the museum is housed, is one of the last structures remaining from the 1939 fair. The building served as the original temporary headquarters of the United Nations General Assembly from 1946 to 1950, when that body was first created. It was here that the historic vote creating the State of Israel was cast in 1947.

The Queens Museum features exhibits ranging from the work of local artists and craftspeople to collections of original works by some of the nation's most renowned artists. But the most celebrated display is the Panorama of New York City, a huge model, on a scale of one inch to 100 feet, showing every major street, building, railroad, bridge, river, park, and highway in the metropolitan area in three-dimensional form. The model was conceived for the 1964 World's Fair. Open Tuesday through Saturday from 10:00 a.m. to 5:00 p.m., Sunday from 1:00 p.m. to 5:00 p.m. Suggested donation is $1. (1)

Leaving the museum, turn LEFT at 1st Street (in the park), along a row of hedges.

1.6 Take the first LEFT at "Boylan Boulevard," passing over a small bridge and heading toward the zoo and Space Park.

Another relic of the 1964 World's Fair, the outdoor display of full-scale models of U.S. spacecraft is now attached to the Hall of Science, a museum with hands-on exhibits of science-related subjects. A section called "Technology of New York City" presents models of city structures and systems, such as a cross-section of the track and ties and signal system from the subway. Open Wednesday through Friday from 10:00 a.m. to 4:00 p.m., Saturday from 10:00 a.m. to 5:00 p.m., and Sunday 11:00 a.m. to 5:00 p.m. Admission is by donation ($2.00 suggested for adults, $1.00 for children). (2)

1.8 Bear LEFT around the domed aviary of the Flushing Meadow Zoo, passing the children's farm on your right. Continue bearing LEFT around the zoo, passing over a bridge, and head for the New York State Pavilion (Theatre in the Park).

2.3 Turn RIGHT just *past* the pavilion. Go past a fountain and over a bridge that spans the Long Island Expressway.

2.7 Turn RIGHT at the end of the bridge, facing the Amphitheater, and continue around the western shore of Meadow Lake.

3.8 When you get to the far end of the lake, exit the park through an opening in the fence opposite the ballfield, and turn RIGHT onto Jewel Avenue, which becomes 69th Road, uphill.

4.5 Turn LEFT at 108th Street.

4.7 At the end of 108th Street, cross Queens Boulevard and pick up Continental Avenue on the other side.

4.9 Turn LEFT at Station Square, a cobblestoned plaza at the entrance to Forest Hills Gardens.

Dominating the square is the towered, turreted Forest Hills Inn, built in 1912 to resemble an Elizabethan country inn. Its rooms and apartments were connected by covered archways to the Long Island Railroad station platform. The inn and its sidewalk café were popular gathering places for tennis fans and players during the National Tennis Championships, which were held in Forest Hills until a few years ago. (3)

5.0 Bear RIGHT, passing underneath an arch, onto Greenway Terrace in Forest Hills Gardens.

Around 1910, the Long Island Railroad sold a tract of land south of its Forest Hills station to the Russell Sage Foundation. Mrs. Sage, widow of the famed New York financier, proceeded to develop the tract in an unusual way. The solid and tasteful construction of the buildings in her development was in striking contrast to the cheaply built structures that characterized most developments in outlying districts at that time. The estatelike homes were originally designed for low- and middle-income families. Ironically, they are now worth up to two million dollars each, making this one of the most exclusive communities in the city. The grounds were landscaped by the Olmstead brothers, of Central Park and Prospect Park fame. (4)

Bear RIGHT, onto Greenway *South.*

5.6 Turn RIGHT at the end, onto Union Turnpike.

5.8 Take the first sharp LEFT at Metropolitan Avenue.

6.0 Turn LEFT at Forest Park Drive.

6.3 Take the first LEFT at Park Lane, then turn LEFT again at the end, onto Union Turnpike.

6.5 Take the second RIGHT at Greenway *North,* going back into Forest Hills Gardens.

6.8 Turn RIGHT at Puritan Avenue.

6.9 Turn LEFT at the end, onto Burns Street.

7.1 **Dogleg RIGHT at Ascan Avenue, to stay on Burns Street.**

7.4 **Cross Continental Avenue and continue STRAIGHT on Burns Street, past the tennis stadium behind a wooden fence on your left.**

Every world-class tennis player alive today has passed through the gates of the elegant Forest Hills Stadium. It was the United States' counterpart to Wimbledon from 1915 until only a few years ago, when the U.S. Open Tennis Championships were moved to a more modern facility in Flushing Meadow Park. The 14.000-seat concrete Forest Hills Stadium has fifty-six courts spread over an area of 10.5 acres. (5)

At the end of the stadium fence, dogleg LEFT to stay on Burns Street.

7.8 **Turn RIGHT at Yellowstone Boulevard.**

8.2 **Cross Queens Boulevard and pick up Jewel Avenue on the other side.**

8.7 **Cross the service road of the Grand Central Parkway and continue onto a bridge that spans the parkway itself.**

Pedal carefully along this stretch, which includes a couple of highway access ramps.

9.0 **At the bottom of the hill, before you reach the traffic light, walk your bike across Jewel Avenue and enter Flushing Meadow Park, on your left, through an opening in the fence. Inside the park, bear RIGHT along the eastern shore of Meadow Lake.**

9.9 **At the opposite end of the lake, cross a channel, then bear RIGHT, and pass underneath a cloverleaf of highways.**

10.3 **Continue bearing RIGHT along the eastern edge of the park next to an elevated highway.**

10.7 **Bear RIGHT again at the next opportunity, so that you pass underneath the elevated highway and then past a ballfield on your left. You will then bike onto a steeply arched concrete bridge that will take you into the grounds of the Queens Botanical Garden.**

11.1 **Once over the bridge, follow the path to the garden's main entrance.**

This recent addition to the Botanical Gardens of New York City holds a wide variety of plant life and landscaping on a small and intimate scale. Among the garden's attractions are the Flowering Cherry Tree Circle, Bee Garden, Rock Garden, Beach Garden, and Pine Cove. The main entrance is at Main Street. (6)

Leaving the Botanical Garden, retrace your path over the steep bridge, back into Flushing Meadow Park. Head for the Unisphere along any of the park paths.

The huge stainless-steel globe, a reminder of the 1964 World's Fair, is generally visible from anywhere in the park.

Unisphere in Flushing Meadow Park.

12.5 From the Unisphere, head for the main entrance of the Queens Museum in the New York City Building. Then turn RIGHT onto the park road, which will take you back to Shea Stadium and the parking field.

Bicycle Shops

Arista Bicycle, Inc., 105-10 Metropolitan Avenue (near Union Turnpike), Forest Hills (718-793-9633)

11

Cemetery Belt

Distance: 11 miles
Terrain: flat
Traffic: moderate

Those who visit the middle of Queens are often struck by one of the borough's most distinctive features: thousands of acres of gravestones cover vast tracts of land, spreading for miles in every direction. In the midnineteenth century, when Manhattan and Brooklyn outlawed the taking of any more land for cemetery purposes, the rush was on to buy up farmland in undeveloped Queens County for burial grounds. Today Queens has twenty-nine cemeteries, ranging in size from one acre to three hundred acres. More space is allotted for this purpose here than in any other part of the city. Most of the cemeteries are located along a band stretching from the Brooklyn-Queens border, northeast into the communities of Middle Village and Maspeth. The region has acquired nicknames such as the *terminal moraine* and *cemetery belt*. Despite the macabre title of this tour, it is a very pleasant short ride on clean streets with evocative names like *dry harbor*, *juniper valley*, and *fresh pond*. The presence of so many graveyards in the area contributes to the tranquillity and seclusion of the surrounding neighborhoods.

While traffic is light in the residential sections, the route does pass through an industrial site where heavy truck traffic is the norm on weekdays. Therefore, weekends are best for this tour. Begin at Woodhaven Boulevard and Dry Harbor Road, a few blocks south of Queens Boulevard, in Middle Village. Drivers, take the Long Island Expressway to Woodhaven Boulevard and go down Woodhaven for about a quarter mile to Dry Harbor Road.

Directions

0.0 Head south on Dry Harbor Road.

The origin of this unusual street name is unclear, but it probably had something to do with the fact that the community of Middle Village was developed on a huge swampland. The infamous bog, called Juniper Swamp, has long since disappeared, but it is remembered in the street names. Many of the older dwellings in the area were built on wooden pilings because of swampy ground conditions. (1)

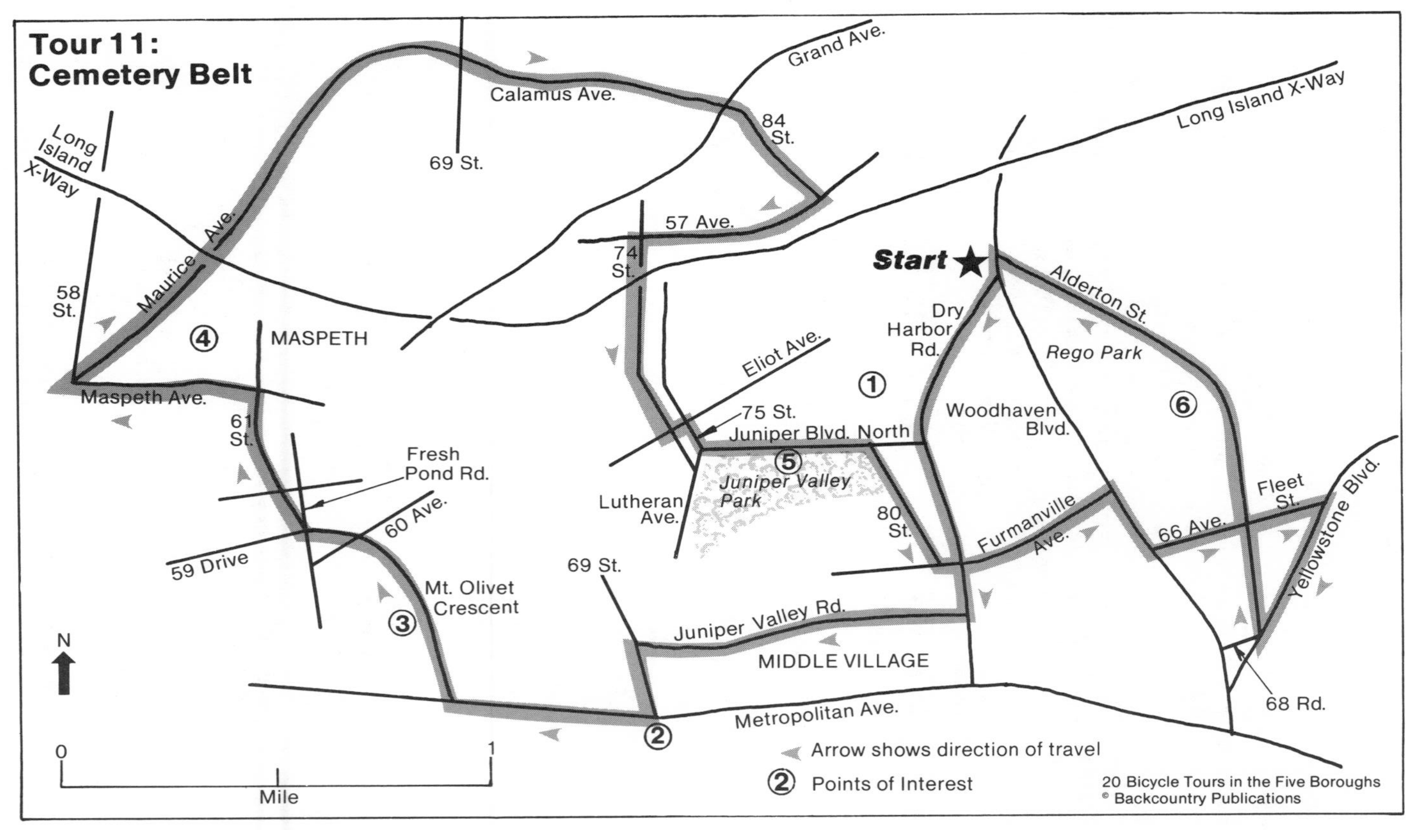
Tour 11:
Cemetery Belt
Grand Ave.
Calamus Ave.
69 St.
84 St.
Long Island X-Way
Long Island X-Way
Maurice Ave.
57 Ave.
74 St.
Start
Alderton St.
Dry Harbor Rd.
Rego Park
58 St.
4
MASPETH
Eliot Ave.
1
6
Maspeth Ave.
75 St.
Woodhaven Blvd.
61 St.
Juniper Blvd. North
5
Fresh Pond Rd.
Juniper Valley Park
Lutheran Ave.
60 Ave.
80 St.
Furmanville Ave.
66 Ave.
Fleet St.
Yellowstone Blvd.
59 Drive
69 St.
Mt. Olivet Crescent
3
Juniper Valley Rd.
MIDDLE VILLAGE
N
68 Rd.
Metropolitan Ave.
2
0
1
Mile
Arrow shows direction of travel
2 Points of Interest
20 Bicycle Tours in the Five Boroughs
© Backcountry Publications

0.9 **Turn RIGHT at Juniper Valley Road.**

1.7 **Turn LEFT at the end, onto 69th Street.**

1.8 **Turn RIGHT at the end, onto Metropolitan Avenue, past Lutheran Cemetery on both your right and your left.**

Middle Village received its name from its geographical position midway between Williamsburg, Brooklyn, and Jamaica, Queens. Metropolitan Avenue, a major thoroughfare linking Queens with Brooklyn and Manhattan, was formerly called the Williamsburg-Jamaica Turnpike. It was a dirt toll road and cost three cents to cross. At the corner of 69th Street and Metropolitan is Neiderstein's, a Middle Village landmark restaurant famous for its architecture as well as its steaks. (2)

2.3 **Turn RIGHT at Mt. Olivet Crescent, past Mt. Olivet Cemetery on your right.**

Obviously many of the businesses in the area are related to burial rites. Florists and tombstone outlets line the street across from the graveyard. A little farther along on the left is the austere Fresh Pond Crematorium. (3)

2.8 **Mt. Olivet Crescent curves to the left and becomes 59th Drive as you cross 60th Avenue.**

2.9 **Turn RIGHT at Fresh Pond Road, then bear LEFT immediately onto 61st Street.**

Around here, traffic builds as you approach industrial areas. Pedal carefully on these narrow, bumpy streets.

3.3 **Turn LEFT at Maspeth Avenue.**

The community of Maspeth, surrounded on three sides by cemeteries, is located at the head of Newtown Creek, the site of the first sizable English settlement in Queens. The name derives from an Indian tribe, the Mespat. Today the area bears a strong industrial character and has been called the Pittsburgh of Queens. Nevertheless, the neighborhood includes lovely residential enclaves that have a small-town flavor. (4)

3.7 **Turn RIGHT at Maurice Avenue.**

Be sure to make a sharp right onto Maurice and not onto 58th Street. As you continue along Maurice, on your left is Mt. Zion Cemetery, and on your right is a row of warehouses. Watch out for trucks pulling in and out of loading platforms.

4.9 **Bear RIGHT onto Calamus Avenue as you cross 68th Street.**

5.6 **Calamus becomes 84th Street as you cross Grand Avenue.**

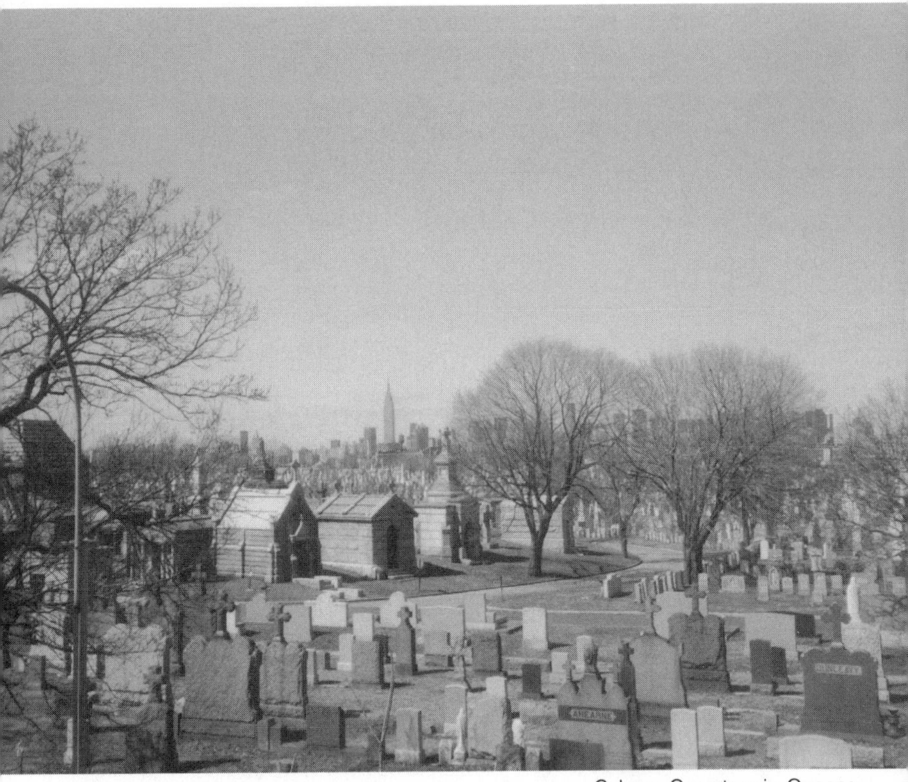

Calvary Cemetery in Queens.

5.9 **Turn RIGHT at the end, onto 57th Avenue, which parallels the Long Island Expressway (LIE).**

6.4 **Turn LEFT at 74th Street, which takes you underneath the LIE.**

6.8 **Turn LEFT at Eliot Avenue. Then turn RIGHT immediately onto Lutheran Avenue.**

6.9 **Bear LEFT onto 75th Street.**

7.0 **Turn LEFT at the end onto unmarked Juniper Boulevard North.**

Juniper Valley Park, on your right, has baseball, football and soccer fields, as well as a roller-hockey rink and bicycle paths. In the middle of the park is a tiny cemetery that has been exposed to vandalism and neglect. But it is left over from earlier days, when the area families would fence off a corner of their farm for private burial grounds. Only a handful of these plots remain, wedged between buildings or hidden on seemingly empty lots. They make a striking contrast to the vast, impersonal plots that cover much of the borough today. (5)

7.4 Take the first RIGHT, at 80th Street.

7.8 Turn LEFT at Furmanville Street.

8.2 Turn RIGHT at busy Woodhaven Boulevard.

8.3 Turn LEFT at 66th Avenue, which becomes Fleet Street.

8.7 Turn RIGHT at Yellowstone Boulevard.

9.0 Take a *sharp* RIGHT at unmarked Alderton Street, just past a railroad overpass.

Make sure you take the sharp right onto Alderton and not onto 68th Road. If you come to Woodhaven Boulevard, you've made the wrong turn. Alderton is the main thoroughfare through Rego Park, a planned community that was laid out and developed by the Real Good Construction Company, whose acronym was adopted for the community's name. Its rowhouses and two- and three-family homes are grouped in an enclave called The Crescents. (6)

10.9 Turn LEFT at Woodhaven Boulevard, and continue for one block back to Dry Harbor Road.

Bicycle Shops

Grand Bicycle Center, 70-13 Grand Avenue, Maspeth (718-429-8204)

G V G Bicycles, Inc., 61-07A 80th Street (off Eliot Avenue), Middle Village (718-478-8177)

Queens Discount Bicycles, 92-94 Queens Boulevard, Rego Park (718-479-3338)

Twin Bicycle and Sporting Goods, 75-20 Metropolitan Avenue, Middle Village (718-326-7725)

12
Archie Bunker Territory

Distance: 11 miles
Terrain: flat
Traffic: moderate

"Boy, the way Glen Miller played . . ." Anyone who has seen the TV series *All in the Family* remembers the two-family wood-frame house pictured during the opening credits of the program. Such houses are so familiar a feature of the Queens landscape that real-estate brokers throughout the borough routinely refer to them as "Archie Bunkers." (And they are a bargain in today's housing market.) Although several Queens neighborhoods claim the distinction of being home to the Bunker family, the Glendale-Ridgewood area seems to fit the bill better than any other. Row upon neat row of Archie Bunker houses line the shaded side streets of these working-class communities near the Brooklyn-Queens border. Most of the homes vary slightly from the TV version, but they all have the same pointed roofs, enclosed porches, and boxy construction.

Farther down the road, in central Ridgewood, the turn-of-the-century brick rowhouses have earned this neighborhood its title as the nation's largest Historic District. Both communities enjoy their proximity to Forest Park, one of the city's most pristine and densely wooded recreation areas. Begin the ride at the intersection of Woodhaven Boulevard and Metropolitan Avenue in the Glendale section of Queens.

Directions

0.0 Head west on Metropolitan Avenue for just two blocks, then take the second LEFT, at Cooper Avenue, along the edge of St. John's Cemetery.

0.6 When you come to a blinking yellow light just past 69th Drive, stay to the left of the light. Go downhill and underneath a railroad overpass.

0.9 Passing 73rd Place, continue STRAIGHT, onto Central Avenue.

Glendale is a quiet, stable, residential working-class neighborhood with a large German-American population. The side streets north and south of Central Avenue abound in examples of the Archie Bunker house in all its variations. (1)

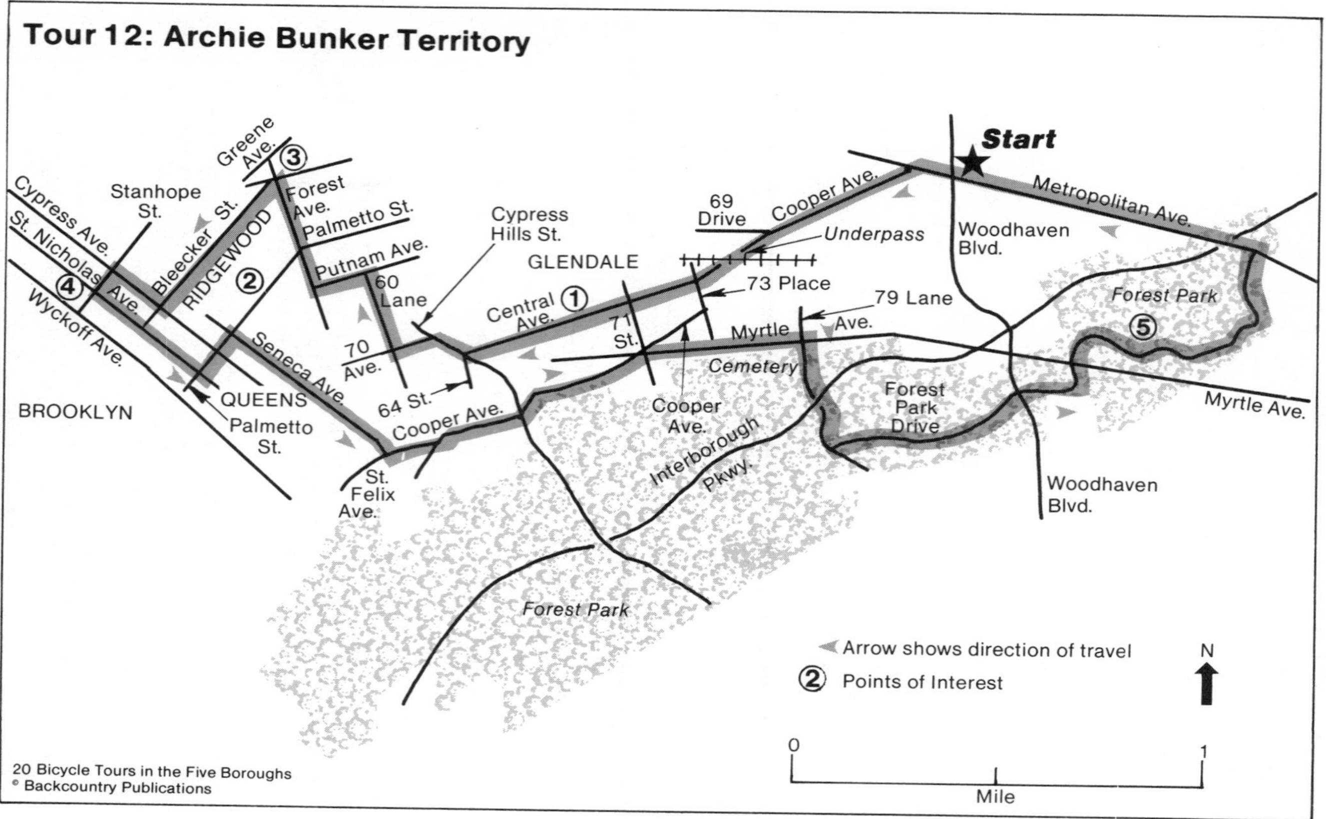
Tour 12: Archie Bunker Territory
Start
Metropolitan Ave.
Woodhaven Blvd.
Forest Park
5
Myrtle Ave.
Woodhaven Blvd.
Cooper Ave.
Underpass
69 Drive
73 Place
79 Lane
Ave.
Myrtle
Cemetery
Forest Park Drive
Cooper Ave.
Interborough Pkwy.
GLENDALE
71 St.
Central Ave.
1
Cypress Hills St.
Forest Park
60 Lane
Forest Ave.
Palmetto St.
Putnam Ave.
70 Ave.
64 St.
Cooper Ave.
St. Felix Ave.
3
Greene Ave.
2
RIDGEWOOD
Seneca Ave.
QUEENS
Palmetto St.
Stanhope St.
Bleecker St.
Cypress Ave.
St. Nicholas Ave.
4
Wyckoff Ave.
BROOKLYN
Arrow shows direction of travel
2 Points of Interest
N
0
1
Mile
20 Bicycle Tours in the Five Boroughs
© Backcountry Publications

1.8 At 64th Street, bear RIGHT onto Cypress Hills Street.

1.9 Take the second LEFT, at 70th Avenue.

2.0 Take the second RIGHT, at 60th *Lane.*

2.3 Turn LEFT at the end, onto Putnam Avenue.

2.5 Turn RIGHT at the end, onto Forest Avenue.

The yellow and tan brick rowhouses of Ridgewood look just as they did when they were built by German immigrants before World War I. The neighborhood was designated a federal Historic District in 1983, replacing Greenwich Village as the largest such district in the nation.

Rowhouses in Ridgewood Historic District.

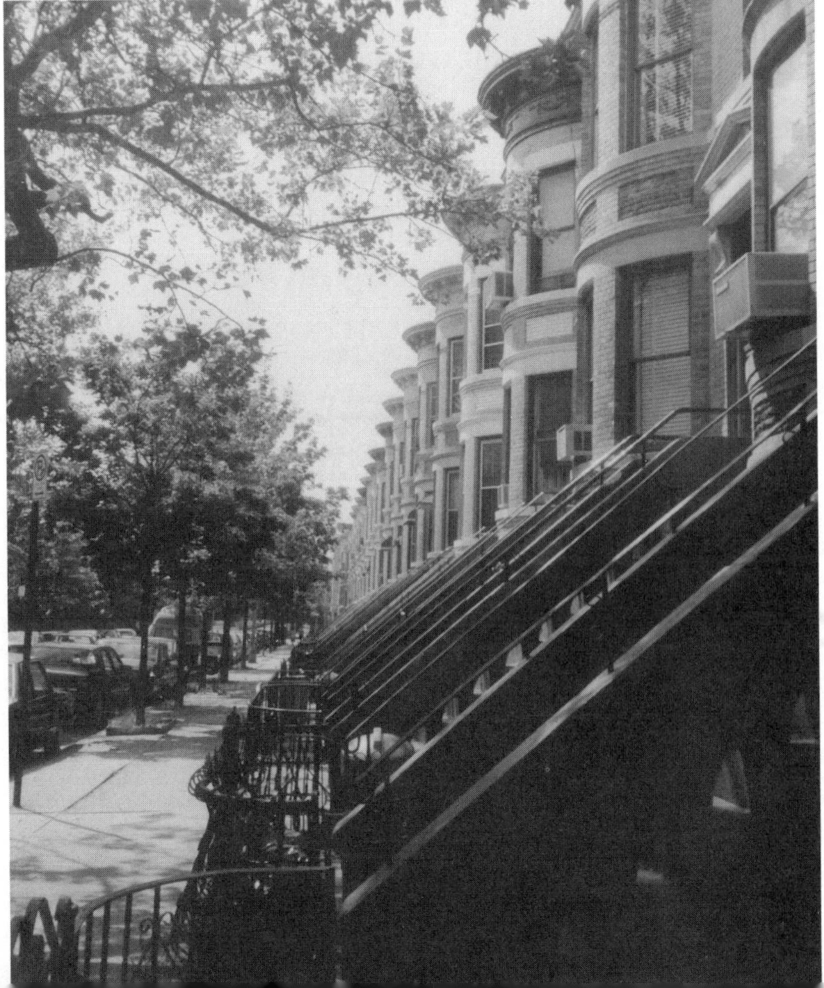

At the turn of the century, immigrants were attracted by jobs in the community's breweries and knitting mills, traces of which still remain in the area. The architectural signature of Ridgewood is the Matthews Flat. According to the Ridgewood Historical Society, these flats were typical turn-of-the-century dwellings for immigrant workers. They were built by the Matthews Company, a firm of three German-born brothers who specialized in building them; they built more than a thousand throughout the neighborhood. Although the buildings all have the same internal layout, the builders "exercised their creativity on the exteriors, which display intricate and variegated brickwork." The buildings have been well-maintained by generations of German housewives. Some of the best examples are on Palmetto Street, just west of Forest Avenue. (2)

2.9 Turn LEFT at Bleecker Street. Bear LEFT immediately after turning, to stay on Bleecker.

Before making the turn at Bleecker, you may want to proceed one block beyond the intersection, to Greene Street. There, set back from the road on the left, is a handsome Tudor structure. It is now a garage, but the building was formerly a stable and is thought to have belonged to one of the community's early twentieth-century breweries. Its fanciful architecture is typical of those breweries, and it is one of few remaining traces of that aspect of the area's history. (3)

3.5 Turn RIGHT at Cypress Avenue.

3.8 Turn LEFT at Stanhope Street, and continue for one block.

3.9 Turn LEFT at St. Nicholas Avenue.

On the northwest corner of Stanhope and St. Nicholas is the Wyckoff Heights General Hospital, an imposing, slightly gloomy structure that looms up like a haunted castle. It was originally called the Deutsche Hospital Gesellschaft, or German Hospital Society of Brooklyn—its name was changed during World War I. It is currently a viable institution with 250 beds. (4)

4.4 Turn LEFT at Palmetto Street, underneath the el.

The elevated subway tracks along Wyckoff Avenue form the boundary between Brooklyn and Queens. Ridgewood residents also hope this boundary line will serve as a symbolic barrier against the encroaching blight of Bushwick, Brooklyn, on the other side of the tracks. In 1979, after a lengthy and much-publicized debate, Ridgewood cut its Zip Code tie to Brooklyn and officially became part of Queens. Before that, half the neighborhood lay in Brooklyn.

4.6 Turn RIGHT at Seneca Avenue.

5.3 Turn LEFT at the end, onto St. Felix Avenue.

Archie Bunker-type houses in Glendale.

5.5 Turn LEFT at the end, onto Cooper Avenue.

Cooper Avenue does not follow a straight course but makes several sharp turns. Follow the green signs to stay on Cooper.

5.9 At Cypress Hills Street, bear LEFT, then RIGHT, to stay on Cooper Avenue.

6.3 At 71st Street, bear RIGHT onto Myrtle Avenue, past a McDonald's on your right.

You should now be riding along a cemetery on your right.

6.9 Turn RIGHT at 79th *Lane* into Forest Park. Stay on Forest Park Drive, avoiding the Interborough Parkway (which is marked by green signs).

7.5 When you come to an intersection at the top of a low hill, bear LEFT, following the signs to the Sueffert Bandshell.
Continue to follow the bandshell signs.

8.3 At the traffic light, cross Woodhaven Boulevard and continue STRAIGHT onto Forest Park Drive.

True to its name, Forest Park encompasses over five hundred acres of dense and possibly virgin woodland in the midst of the city. In summer the canopy of vegetation is so thick that sunlight barely penetrates. The park lies along the top of a ridge created by the glacial moraine that forms the backbone of Long Island, so the terrain is rolling. In addition to the low hills, steep-sided pits, flat plains, and rock fragments carried here by the Wisconsin Glacier ten thousand years ago, the park contains a number of *kettle holes.* A kettle hole is a depression in the land that was formed when chunks of ice were overridden and buried by glacial debris. When the ice chunks melted, the debris above them sank into the mud, creating "kettles." Often the type of plant life that covers them is different from that of their surroundings.

Forest Park Drive east of Woodhaven Boulevard is closed to automobile traffic on weekends between 10:00 A.M. and 4:00 P.M., and also on weekdays during the summer months. (5)

Continue STRAIGHT along Forest Park Drive to the next traffic light.

9.7 Turn LEFT at the traffic light, onto Metropolitan Avenue, and continue for about 1.5 miles back to the starting point at Woodhaven Boulevard.

Bicycle Shops

Arista Bicycle, Inc., 105-10 Metropolitan Avenue, Forest Hills (718-793-9633)
Expressway Bicycles, 801 Cypress Avenue, Ridgewood (718-417-1688)

13
Getaway

Distance: 20 miles
Terrain: flat
Traffic: light

Just a few miles from the "concrete jungle" and congestion of midtown Manhattan lies a twenty-thousand-acre natural area that comprises this nation's first national park within a city: the Gateway National Recreation Area. A wildlife refuge, miles of seashore, two defunct military installations, and a couple of unique residential communities are among the attractions you'll sample on this long and diversified tour of the Jamaica Bay and Breezy Point units of the GNRA. You'll seldom lose sight of water on this trip. The marinas of Howard Beach are followed by the bird-rich wetlands of Jamaica Bay and the Rockaway Peninsula seashore. Then come unobstructed views of the bay from a city bicycle path that runs beside the Belt Parkway between Brooklyn and Queens. The National Park Service has taken over two inactive military bases in the area and highlighted their historical significance as part of the nation's early coastal defense system: Fort Tilden and Floyd Bennett Field offer rare opportunities to observe a disappearing phenomenon.

This route offers a unique combination of natural and cultural features and is especially accommodating to the bicycle tourist. It is best in the fall, when the beach crowds are gone and the ocean breezes are at their balmiest. The tour begins at 157th Avenue and Cross Bay Boulevard in the Howard Beach section of Queens. Drivers take the Belt Parkway to Cross Bay Boulevard *South*. 157th Avenue is just south of the parkway.

Directions

0.0 Head south on Cross Bay Boulevard. At 0.8 mile cross the North Channel Bridge, which spans the portion of Jamaica Bay between Howard Beach and Broad Channel Island.

The bridge is a popular fishing spot in the summer. If you use the walkway, you'll be dodging buckets and poles, not to mention tangled fish lines and rusty hooks. It's better to stay on the roadway, hugging the right as closely as possible to avoid fast-moving traffic.

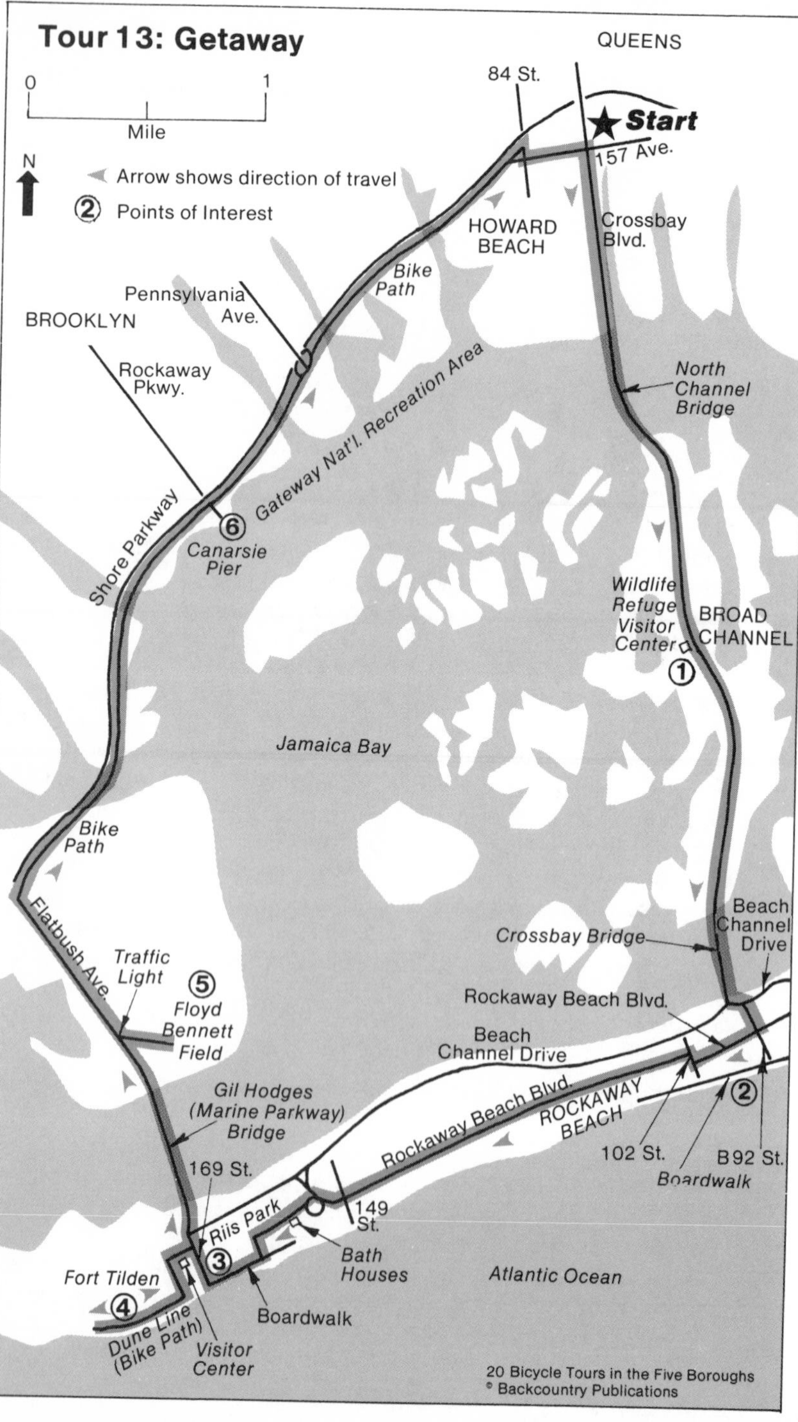

Tour 13: Getaway
0
1
Mile
N
Arrow shows direction of travel
② Points of Interest
QUEENS
84 St.
Start
157 Ave.
HOWARD BEACH
Crossbay Blvd.
Bike Path
Pennsylvania Ave.
BROOKLYN
Rockaway Pkwy.
Gateway Nat'l. Recreation Area
North Channel Bridge
Shore Parkway
⑥
Canarsie Pier
Wildlife Refuge Visitor Center
BROAD CHANNEL
①
Jamaica Bay
Bike Path
Beach Channel Drive
Crossbay Bridge
Flatbush Ave.
Traffic Light
⑤
Floyd Bennett Field
Rockaway Beach Blvd.
Beach Channel Drive
Gil Hodges (Marine Parkway) Bridge
Rockaway Beach Blvd.
ROCKAWAY BEACH
②
102 St.
B92 St.
Boardwalk
169 St.
Riis Park
149 St.
③
Bath Houses
Atlantic Ocean
Fort Tilden
④
Dune Line (Bike Path)
Visitor Center
Boardwalk
20 Bicycle Tours in the Five Boroughs
© Backcountry Publications

2.0 Having crossed the North Channel Bridge, continue STRAIGHT on Cross Bay Boulevard, through the Jamaica Bay Wildlife Refuge.

A haven for at least two hundred species of birds, including twenty-four varieties of waterfowl, these marshlands are noted for the robust health of their ecological systems amid unhealthy urban environmental conditions. The area is especially exciting during the fall migration season, when thousands of ducks and geese on the Atlantic Flyway stop over on the two refuge ponds. A one-and-a-half-mile hiking trail takes walkers through part of the marshlands and around a man-made freshwater pond. Bicycle racks, free hiking permits, and information are available at the Visitor Center, on your right at the south end of the preserve. (1)

3.2 Leaving the wildlife refuge, turn RIGHT on to Cross Bay Boulevard. Continue STRAIGHT, through the community of Broad Channel.

Home to about a thousand families, some of whom appear to be living in ramshackle houses set on stilts at the water's edge, Broad Channel is the only settlement on the islands of Jamaica Bay.

4.5 As you approach the Cross Bay Veterans Memorial Bridge, cross the boulevard to pick up the walkway, which is on your left as you face the bridge.

This is another popular fishing spot. But here you have no choice but to use the walkway—cyclists are forbidden to use the roadway.

5.3 Coming off the bridge in Rockaway Beach, turn LEFT at Beach Channel Drive. Then take the first RIGHT at B 92nd Street.

5.5 Turn RIGHT at Rockaway Beach Boulevard.

Once one of the city's most elegant seaside resorts, Rockaway's reputation is somewhat jaded today, and the community is rundown. However, the surf is still inviting and the beach has recently been the focus of large-scale antierosion efforts to restore a disappearing coastline. (2)

The Beach and boardwalk are two blocks to the left of Rockaway Beach Boulevard.

Continue STRAIGHT (westbound) on Rockaway Beach Boulevard.

6.1 Dogleg one block to the RIGHT at 102nd Street to stay on Rockaway Beach Boulevard.

For the next 2.5 miles, you pass through the progressively more attractive communities of Rockaway Park, Belle Harbor, and Neponsit.

8.2 Just past 149th Street, Rockaway Beach Boulevard curves to the right, then forks. Take the LEFT fork, halfway around a traffic circle, following the signs to Riis Park. Continue STRAIGHT, past the bathhouses on your left.

Rockaway Beach.

Jacob Riis Park was named after the crusading journalist who battled for better recreation facilities and housing at the turn of the century. Its beach is considered one of the finest ocean beaches in the metropolitan region. The old brick art-deco bathhouses are city landmarks. (3)

A different kind of crusade took place here more recently: a controversial nudist beach abutting the stodgy, well-heeled community of Neponsit made Riis Park a hot news item every summer for several years. The nudism was finally outlawed after a long battle with the community residents.

8.7 At the end of the road, just past the bathhouse on your left and a parking field on your right, turn LEFT onto a walkway, then RIGHT onto the concrete "boardwalk," passing a tall clock on your left.

9.0 Turn RIGHT at the end of the "boardwalk," onto unmarked 169th Street.

9.2 Turn LEFT into the main entrance to Fort Tilden, passing the Visitor Center on your left.

This largely inactive military installation provides a rare opportunity to observe at close range the paraphernalia that once constituted part of our nation's coastal defense system. Missile emplacements, batteries, ammunition sheds, and radar bases are being restored here by the National Park Service and can be viewed from a bicycle path along dunes that once served as camouflage for the equipment. Also of interest here is a "dune restoration" project intended to revive an important element of the coastal ecology. To fully appreciate the area, stop in at the Visitor Center for maps and information. (4)

To get to the dunes, follow the road past the Visitor Center, chapel, and barracks. Turn LEFT at the end, then RIGHT onto a lonely stretch through the dunes.

11.0 Retrace your path to the Fort Tilden main entrance. Leaving Fort Tilden, turn LEFT at 169th Street.

11.1 Cross Beach Channel Drive and pick up the pedestrian path of the Gil Hodges Memorial Bridge (also called the Marine Parkway Bridge).

11.8 Coming off the bridge, continue STRAIGHT along the Flatbush Avenue bike route to the first traffic light.

12.0 Turn RIGHT at the traffic light, crossing Flatbush Avenue, into Floyd Bennett Field.

This immense airfield, almost twice the size of Central Park, has a colorful history as the city's first municipal airport. It was here that Wiley Post took off and landed aboard the *Winnie Mae* in making the first solo flight around the world in 1933. After the U.S. Navy took over the airfield, aviation history continued to be made here with the record-breaking speed flights of test pilot (and future astronaut) John Glenn. You can cycle along the abandoned runways where illustrious pilots like Roscoe Turner, Amelia Earhart, and Howard Hughes took off; and you'll pass a strip of dilapidated buildings known as Hangar Row. For more information, stop in at Park Headquarters in Building 69, inside the main entrance. (5)

Leave Floyd Bennett Field, and turn RIGHT at Flatbush Avenue.

12.9 Just *before* you reach the access ramp to the Belt Parkway East-

bound, turn RIGHT onto the bicycle path that runs alongside the parkway. Continue eastbound on the bike path.

Soon you pass the Jamaica Bay Riding Academy on your right at Bergen Beach.

16.4 Turn RIGHT at Rockaway Parkway onto Canarsie Pier.

Canarsie Pier is the lone remnant of a 1920s scheme to fill in part of Jamaica Bay and create a full-scale harbor there. The pier was the first stage of the project; it was completed in 1927 at a cost of $500,000. Fortunately the plan was abandoned, but this concrete slab remains as a monument to grandiose and ill-fated schemes in this city's history. (6)

Leaving the pier, turn RIGHT onto the bicycle path and resume riding eastbound along the Belt Parkway.

17.7 Just past Pennsylvania Avenue, the bicycle path begins to deteriorate badly.

Those with very sturdy or all-terrain bikes can continue to pedal. Others will probably have to walk for about 0.5 mile until the path improves again, before it reaches Cross Bay Boulevard.

19.7 Turn RIGHT at 84th Street, leaving the bike path.

19.8 Take the first LEFT at 157th Avenue, which will take you back to the start at Cross Bay Boulevard.

Bicycle Shops

Harbor Bicycles, 115-06 Beach Channel Drive, Rockaway Park (718-318-0377)

Bikes and Things, 108-13 Rockaway Beach Boulevard, Rockaway Park (718-318-1964)

14
Ray's Loop

Distance: 16 miles
Terrain: flat
Traffic: light

Pedaling in the Marine Park section of Brooklyn one day, I came across some markings on the ground that were obviously intended for bicycle riders. Painted in black at regular intervals along a bike route were the words *Ray's Loop*, or *RL*, followed by an arrow. I followed the trail until the markings faded and disappeared, leading nowhere. I never found out who Ray was or where his mysterious trail led; but continuing to pedal in a westerly direction, I did uncover some marvelous cycling territory in the outer reaches of the borough, where the city's rat race seems strangely suspended. This tour takes in some of Brooklyn's most colorful neighborhoods—Sheepshead Bay, Coney Island, Brighton Beach—as well as some lesser-known ones, such as a tiny Historic District beneath the tracks of the MacDonald Avenue El. Whether you lunch on fresh catch of the day at Sheepshead Bay, snack on a hot dog at Nathan's Famous on Coney Island, or dine on chicken Kiev in Brighton Beach's "Little Odessa," you'll swallow a mouthful of traditional New York on this fun-filled tour. Thanks, Ray.

The ride begins in Marine Park at Flatbush Avenue and Hendrickson Place, two blocks south of Avenue U, across the street from the King's Plaza Shopping Center. This is just off the Flatbush Avenue (north) exit of the Belt Parkway.

Directions

0.0 **Head south (away from King's Plaza) on the "bike route" along Flatbush Avenue for about a mile, past a golf course and a police station.**

1.2 **Cross the Belt Parkway, but *before* you come to the first traffic light, turn RIGHT onto the bikeway that runs alongside the Belt Parkway, facing traffic.**

The tall grasses along the bikeway to your left are part of the protected wetlands of Gateway National Recreation Area. They are home to many migratory birds and nesting waterfowl. This section of Gateway includes Plumb Beach, a small, secluded beach on Rock-

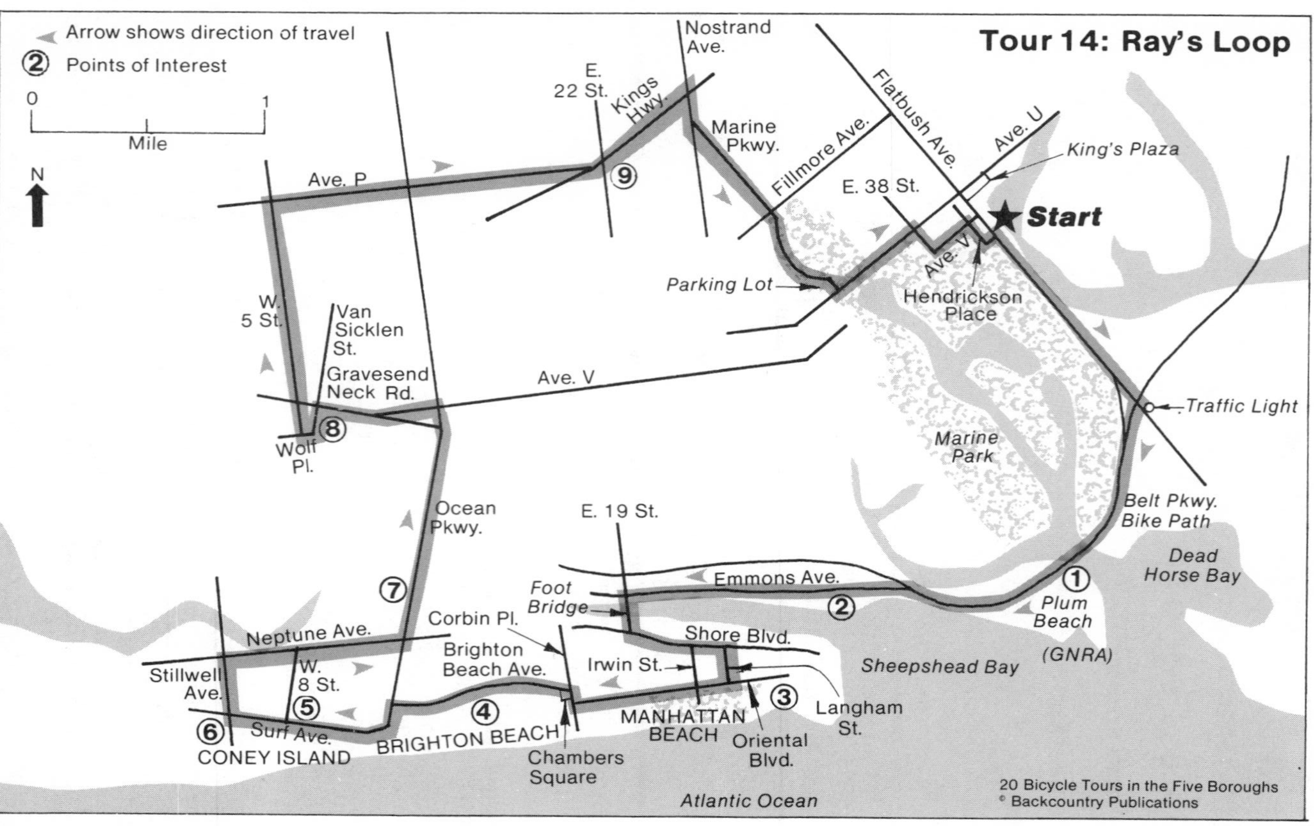

Tour 14: Ray's Loop
Arrow shows direction of travel
② Points of Interest
0
1
Mile
N
Nostrand Ave.
E. 22 St.
Kings Hwy.
Marine Pkwy.
Fillmore Ave.
Flatbush Ave.
Ave. U
King's Plaza
E. 38 St.
Start
Ave. P
Parking Lot
Ave. V
Hendrickson Place
W. 5 St.
Van Sicklen St.
Gravesend Neck Rd.
Ave. V
Traffic Light
Wolf Pl.
Marine Park
Ocean Pkwy.
E. 19 St.
Belt Pkwy. Bike Path
Dead Horse Bay
Foot Bridge
Emmons Ave.
Plum Beach
Corbin Pl.
Shore Blvd.
Neptune Ave.
Brighton Beach Ave.
Irwin St.
Sheepshead Bay
(GNRA)
Stillwell Ave.
W. 8 St.
Langham St.
Surf Ave.
BRIGHTON BEACH
MANHATTAN BEACH
Oriental Blvd.
CONEY ISLAND
Chambers Square
Atlantic Ocean
20 Bicycle Tours in the Five Boroughs
© Backcountry Publications

away Inlet, and Dead Horse Bay, an inlet shaped like a horse's head. The spit of land across the bay is Breezy Point, also a part of Gateway. (1)

3.1 At the end of the bicycle path, turn LEFT onto Emmons Avenue in Sheepshead Bay.

Sheepshead Bay means "fishing" and "seafood" to most New Yorkers. Docked at the marina along Emmons Avenue is a fleet of fishing boats, available for hire. They start early in the morning for fishing expeditions in the surrounding waters and return later in the afternoon to hawk their catches along the piers. The Lundy Brothers restaurant, a New York seafood tradition for many years, is closed, but dozens of reasonably priced restaurants and open-air food stalls line the waterfront. (2)

4.0 Turn LEFT at East 19th Street, onto a footbridge.

The footbridge at Sheepshead Bay.

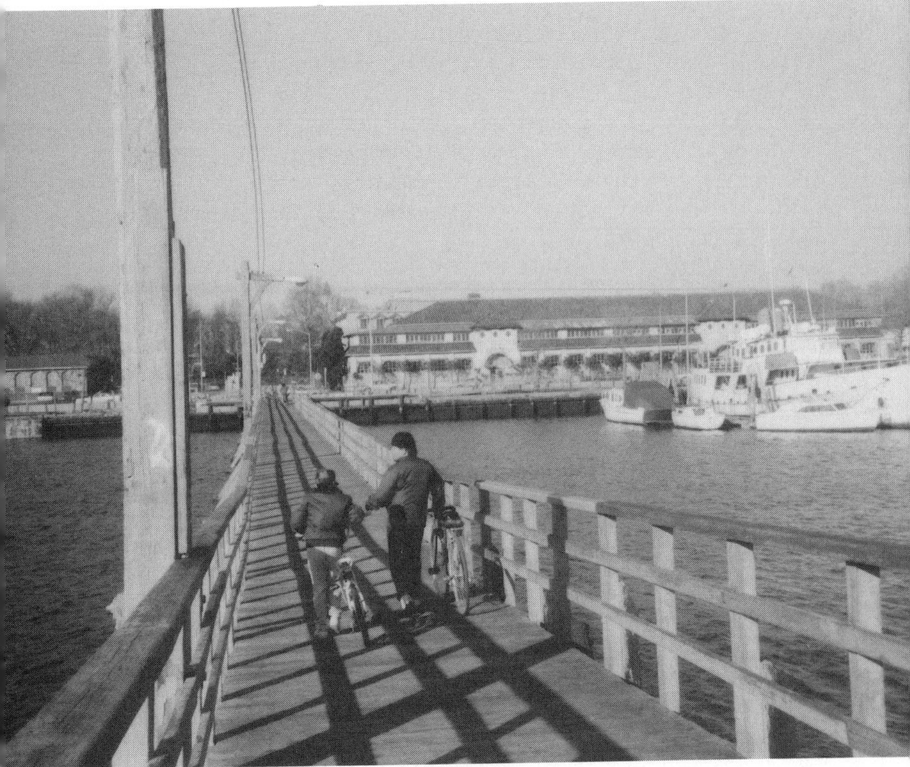

4.1 Turn LEFT at the end of the bridge, onto Shore Boulevard, the waterfront esplanade in Manhattan Beach.

The secluded, well-heeled community of Manhattan Beach occupies the peninsula of what was formerly part of Coney Island. At the eastern tip of the peninsula is the campus of Kingsborough Community College; on the Atlantic side is Manhattan Beach, one of the most pleasant of the city's "subway beaches." (3)

4.6 Turn RIGHT at Langham Street.

4.8 Turn RIGHT at Oriental Boulevard.

4.9 Turn LEFT at Irwin Street, for the beach. Leaving the beach, turn LEFT, back onto Oriental Boulevard.

5.6 Turn RIGHT at the end, onto Corbin Place.

5.7 Take the first LEFT, at the end, onto Chambers Square, which becomes Brighton Beach Avenue.

Continuing along Brooklyn's string of shorefront communities, you are now entering Brighton Beach, one of the city's most solidly ethnic communities. The recent influx of thousands of Russian immigrants has earned this neighborhood the nickname "Little Odessa by the Sea." The Russian presence is muted during the summer by the throngs of beachgoers. But off season, one can spot fur hats and babushkas; food stores selling kasha, caviar, and five-pound loaves of black bread; and restaurants featuring dishes such as chicken Kiev, hot borscht, and *varinikis,* washed down with glasses of cold vodka. (4)

6.6 Turn LEFT at Ocean Parkway, which swings right and becomes Surf Avenue in Coney Island.

The New York Aquarium, on your left at West 8th Street, features whales, seahorses, penguins, octopi, sea anemones, electric eels, and more, all housed in a clean, attractive museum-park environment. Among the most popular attractions are the dolphin and sea lion shows (summer only) and the feeding times for the penguins, seals, whales, and sharks. Open Monday through Friday from 10:00 a.m. to 5:00 p.m.; Saturday, Sunday, and holidays 10:00 a.m. to 6:00 p.m. Admission is $3.75 for adults, 75¢ for children. (5)

7.6 Turn RIGHT at Stillwell Avenue.

The Coney Island amusement area, once touted as the world's greatest, has lost much of its glitter, but quite a few rides and games remain. And Nathan's Famous, at the corner of Stillwell Avenue, still stands as Coney's most immortal institution, dishing up those "famous" frankfurters, french fries, clams on the half-shell, spare ribs, "shrimp boats," and more. (6)

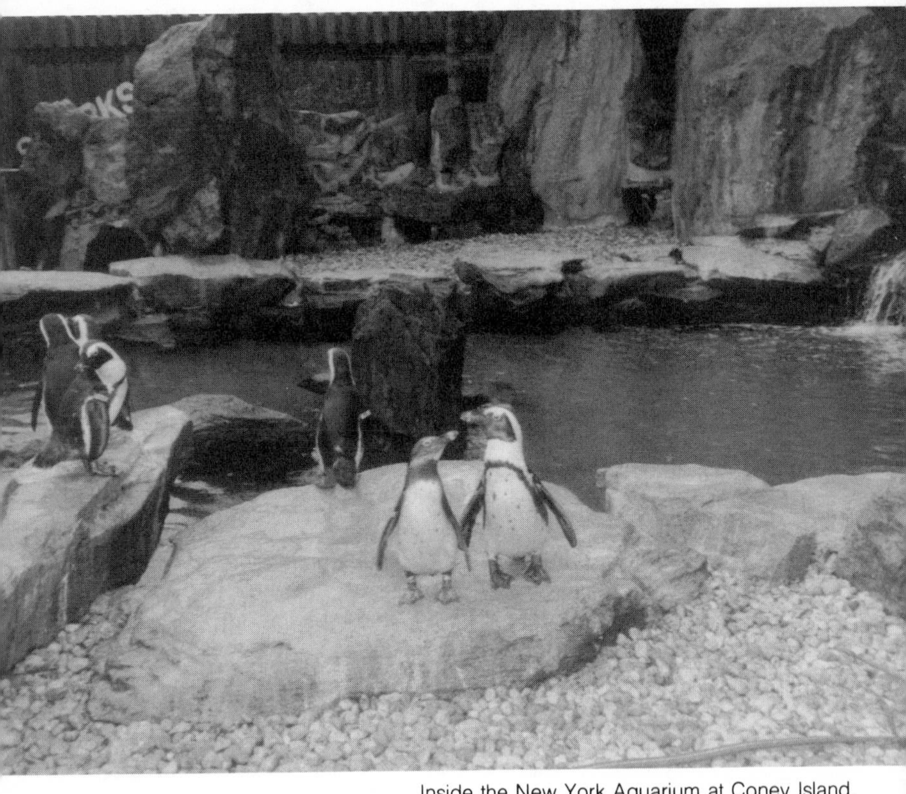

Inside the New York Aquarium at Coney Island.

7.9 Turn RIGHT at Neptune Avenue.

8.6 Turn LEFT at Ocean Parkway.

The pedestrian/bike mall on the southbound side of the parkway is a favorite of Brooklyn cyclists, extending for nearly five miles through the heart of the borough. (7)

9.8 Turn LEFT at Avenue V, which merges into Gravesend Neck Road.

10.3 Turn LEFT at Van Siclen Street.

The tiny landmark Gravesend Cemetery, on your left, is at the corner of a unique historic district, the Old Village of Gravesend. Gravesend was the only one of Brooklyn's original six towns to be settled by the English, not by the Dutch. The village was formally planned in the manner of English colonial towns, with a central square. Now all that remains of the original town plan is the square layout of the blocks bounded by Village Road North, Village Road East, Village Road South, and Van Siclen Street. This is not a historic district in the ordinary sense, but the very observant will notice something different about the place. (8)

10.4 Turn RIGHT at Wolf Place. Take the first RIGHT at West 5th Street.

11.5 Turn RIGHT at Avenue P.

13.0 At East 22nd Street, bear left onto King's Highway.

On the southeast corner at East 22nd Street and Avenue P stands a Dutch Colonial farmhouse dating back to 1766. The Wyckoff-Bennett House is the finest such house still standing in Brooklyn. Its overhanging eaves, six-columned porch, picket fence, and ample grounds and trees are truly anomalous in this unaesthetic section of Brooklyn. The house is privately owned and inhabited, not open to the public. (9)

Continue east on King's Highway.

13.5 Turn RIGHT at Nostrand Avenue.

13.6 Take the first LEFT, at Marine Parkway.

14.2 At the end of Marine Parkway, cross Fillmore Avenue and continue STRAIGHT into the park; then turn RIGHT, onto the circular bikeway. At the opposite end of the park, exit the park through a small parking lot and turn LEFT onto Avenue U.

15.2 Take the first RIGHT, at East 38th Street.

15.3 Turn LEFT at the end, onto Avenue V, then take the first RIGHT at Hendrickson Place, which will lead you back to the starting point at Flatbush Avenue.

Bicycle Shops

Sheepshead Cycle, 2679 Coney Island Avenue (at the corner of Avenue X), Sheepshead Bay (718-648-1440)

Sizzling Bicycle, Inc., 3100 Ocean Parkway (near Brighton Beach Avenue), Brighton Beach (718-372-8985)

Marine Park Bikes, 2913 Quentin Road (between Nostrand and East 29th), Marine Park (718-258-3612)

15

Brooklyn, U.S.A.

Distance: 13 miles
Terrain: flat
Traffic: moderate

Brooklyn used to greet motorists coming off the Brooklyn Bridge with a sign that read, "Welcome to the Nation's Second Largest City." The sign was removed years ago, when the billing was no longer accurate. But with a population of 2.5 million (within an area of seventy-eight square miles), it can't be very far from the truth even now. In view of this density, it is remarkable that some of the best cycling in the city turns up in Brooklyn. The attractive residential section of the borough where this tour begins is hardly a scene of concrete and congestion, as the statistics might suggest. Large old homes on huge lots line the clean wide streets of the Midwood and Flatbush sections near Brooklyn College. Farther along the route, this suburban scene gives way to a more urban landscape. The houses get smaller and closer together and finally yield to the brick rowhouses of Borough Park and the stately brownstones of Park Slope. In the midst of it all is Brooklyn's own celebrated urban oasis, Prospect Park. The park's roadways (traffic-free on weekends) wind around 526 acres of rolling meadows, woods, and lakes, attracting cyclists from miles around. This tour is a true Brooklyn sampler; it passes through a variety of contrasting neighborhoods and provides a bird's-eye view of what the borough is all about.

Begin the ride at the campus of Brooklyn College, deep in the heart of Flatbush, at the intersection of Bedford Avenue and Campus Road, one block south of Glenwood Road. If you plan to drive to the site on a weekday (which is *not* recommended), bring a supply of quarters to feed the six-hour parking meters around the college. Parking is free—and much more available—on weekends.

Directions

0.0 Head south (the house numbers are increasing) on Bedford Avenue.

1.2 Turn RIGHT at Avenue O.

1.7 Turn RIGHT at East 17th Street.

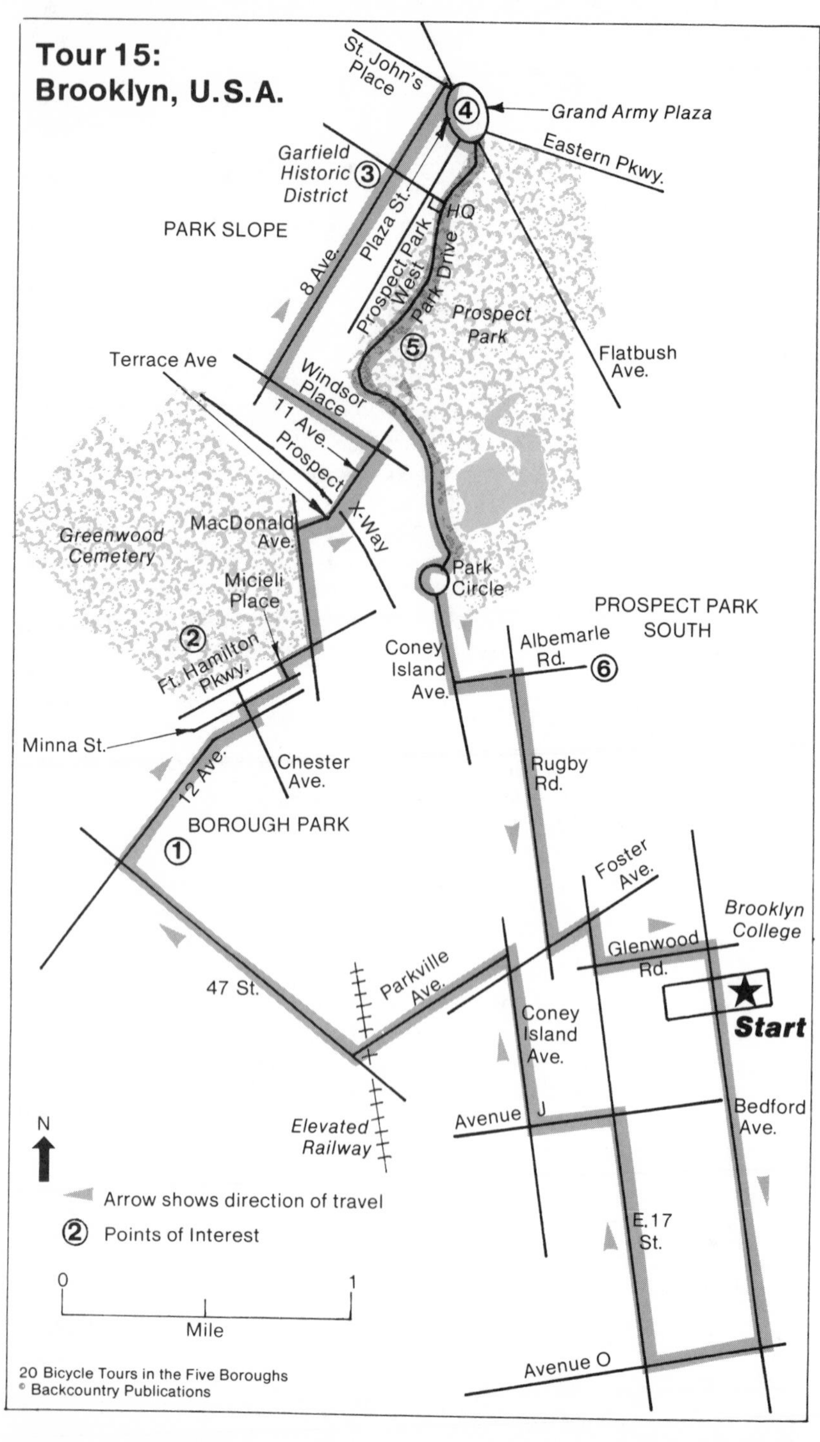
Tour 15:
Brooklyn, U.S.A.
St. John's Place
Grand Army Plaza
Eastern Pkwy.
Garfield Historic District
PARK SLOPE
8 Ave.
Plaza St.
HQ
Prospect Park West
Park Drive
Prospect Park
Flatbush Ave.
Terrace Ave
Windsor Place
11 Ave.
Prospect
X-Way
Greenwood Cemetery
MacDonald Ave.
Micieli Place
Park Circle
PROSPECT PARK SOUTH
Ft. Hamilton Pkwy.
Coney Island Ave.
Albemarle Rd.
Minna St.
Chester Ave.
12 Ave.
Rugby Rd.
BOROUGH PARK
Foster Ave.
Brooklyn College
Glenwood Rd.
Parkville Ave.
47 St.
Coney Island Ave.
Start
Elevated Railway
Avenue J
Bedford Ave.
N
Arrow shows direction of travel
Points of Interest
E.17 St.
0
1
Mile
Avenue O
20 Bicycle Tours in the Five Boroughs
© Backcountry Publications

2.5 **Turn LEFT at Avenue J.**

2.8 **Turn RIGHT at Coney Island Avenue.**

This is a very busy thoroughfare with fast-moving, aggressive traffic.

3.4 **Turn LEFT at Parkville Avenue, which is on your left only, one block past Foster Avenue.**

4.0 **Turn RIGHT at 47th Street, one block past the elevated railway.**

5.5 **Turn RIGHT at 12th Avenue.**

The endless rows of two- and three-story brick dwellings may seem monotonous, but this is no ordinary neighborhood. Borough Park is home to the largest concentration of Orthodox Jews outside Israel, and it continues to attract large numbers of a particular sect, mostly from Eastern Europe. The commercial strips along the avenues exhibit more signs in Hebrew than in English and, as in Williamsburg, the whole neighborhood is eerily deserted on Saturday afternoons, except for residents heading for synagogue dressed in traditional garb. (1)

5.8 **Turn LEFT at Chester Avenue. Then take the first RIGHT at Minna Street.**

6.0 **Turn LEFT at Micieli Place. Then turn RIGHT at the end, onto Fort Hamilton Parkway, opposite the entrance to Greenwood Cemetery.**

Greenwood Cemetery rivals the Bronx's Woodlawn Cemetery as a resting place for the city's illustrious and elite. "Boss" Tweed, Horace Greeley, DeWitt Clinton, and Lola Montez are among its posthumous inhabitants. Behind the ornate gatehouse across from Micieli Place lie twenty-two miles of winding paths on 478 acres of beautifully landscaped wooded hills, ponds, and family plots with fanciful mausoleums and tombstones. The grounds are open to the public for strolling. (2)

6.2 **Take the first LEFT at McDonald Avenue, along the western edge of Greenwood Cemetery.**

6.6 **Turn RIGHT at Terrace Place, one block past Seeley Avenue. Terrace Place becomes 11th Avenue as you cross the Prospect Expressway.**

7.0 **Turn LEFT at Windsor Place.**

7.4 **Turn RIGHT at Eighth Avenue.**

Attention brownstone buffs: After passing through a rather shabby area along Eighth Avenue, you'll enter a designated Historic District that encompasses one of the nation's highest concentrations of Victorian architecture and some of the most magnificent brownstones in the city. As recently as the 1970s, the neighborhood of Park Slope was on the verge of succumbing to urban blight, but the

Historic District designation led to the "gentrification" and renovation of its neglected buildings. The tasteful Park Slope townhouses are famous for the quality of their external detailing. The best examples are along the side streets east and west of Eighth Avenue, after passing Garfield Place. Take some time to explore the neighborhood. (3)

8.6 Turn RIGHT at St. John's Place. Then take the first RIGHT at Plaza Street West.

8.8 Cross Prospect Park West. Then enter Prospect Park through the stone pillars on the right.

Before entering the park, stop to admire the landmark Soldiers' and

Soldiers and Sailors Monument at Grand Army Plaza.

Fountain at Grand Army Plaza.

Sailors' Memorial Arch in Grand Army Plaza. The monument is dedicated to the men who fought in the Union Army during the Civil War. A walk around Grand Army Plaza, which was modeled after Paris's Place de l'Etoile, will reveal a number of smaller but equally impressive monuments and statues. (4)

8.9 After entering Prospect Park, bear RIGHT onto the park drive that runs along the park's western edge.

This urban oasis, designed in 1866 by master landscape architects

Frederick Law Olmsted and Calvert Vaux, is said to surpass their other creation, Central Park, in beauty and architectural interest. The park's 526 acres of meadows, woods, and lakes conceal a wealth of attractions, including an eighteenth-century Dutch farmhouse, the famous Camperdown Elm tree, and a historic Quaker burial ground that was established in 1846, before the park was built. Of course, to explore these offerings you will have to leave the park drive and venture inland along the maze of paths and walkways that crisscross the landscape. For those who wish to do so, maps are available at the park's headquarters in the Litchfield Mansion, which is visible to your right shortly after you enter the park. (5)

10.6 Exit the park drive at Coney Island Avenue.

10.7 Coming out of the park, bear RIGHT at the traffic light. Go halfway around Park Circle, then turn RIGHT at Coney Island Avenue.

Remember, this is a very busy, hazardous street for cyclists.

11.1 Turn LEFT at Albemarle Road (which is on your left only), just past Church Avenue.

Leaving behind the traffic and sprawl of Coney Island Avenue, suddenly you're in a hamlet of turn-of-the-century Colonial and Victorian houses with wraparound porches, columns, towers, and turrets. How did this enclave escape the high-rise development and urban sprawl of the surrounding area? Nobody really knows. The neighborhood, known as Prospect Park South, has been designated a Historic District, but it remains something of an enigma to historians. Those who explore the neighborhood will find some extraordinary architecture here. (6)

11.3 Turn RIGHT at Rugby Road.

12.2 Turn LEFT at Foster Avenue.

12.3 Turn RIGHT at East 17th Street.

12.5 Turn LEFT at Glenwood Road.

12.9 Turn RIGHT at Bedford Avenue, back to Brooklyn College.

Bicycle Shops

Ace Cycles, 1120 Cortelyou Road (near Coney Island Avenue), Flatbush (718-462-7713)

Arnold's Bicycles, 4216 Eighth Avenue, Sunset Park (718-435-8558)

Bicycle Land, 424 Coney Island Avenue (near Prospect Park) (718-633-0820)

Big Wheels, 3006 Avenue L (near Nostrand Avenue) (718-377-4982)

Brooklyn Bicycle Center, 715 Coney Island Avenue (near Beverley Road) (718-941-9095)

R & A Cycles, 101-105 Fifth Avenue (corner of Park Place), Park Slope (718-638-9479; 718-636-5242)

16
Bike Fever

Distance: 13 miles
Terrain: flat
Traffic: moderate

Back in 1978, when John Travolta, as Tony Manero, performed his awesome dance routine at a neighborhood disco in the movie *Saturday Night Fever,* he put Bay Ridge, Brooklyn, on the map. The handsome hero strutted down local streets and cavorted with friends on the nearby Verrazano-Narrows Bridge. A generation earlier, in the neighboring community of Bensonhurst, Jackie Gleason, as Ralph Kramden, bickered endlessly with his wife Alice in the legendary TV series *The Honeymooners*. Bay Ridge and Bensonhurst have been immortalized by show business. Both neighborhoods were chosen as the locales for their respective productions because they were thought to embody the true "spirit of Brooklyn."

But for those who are not especially turned on by movie trivia, this tour of southwestern Brooklyn offers many other interesting diversions. A four-mile bicycle path that runs along the Narrows—the channel that separates Brooklyn from Staten Island—provides some dazzling views of New York Bay, Staten Island, and the Verrazano Bridge; and Fort Hamilton, at the foot of the bridge, is the site of a museum commemorating our region's coastal defense history. On this ride the terrain should present no problem, but the weather might. Even a moderate breeze can seem an irresistible force as it funnels through the Narrows between Upper and Lower New York Bay. For an easier ride, choose a calm, windless day.

The route begins and ends at Bensonhurst Park, at the foot of Bay Parkway (exit 5), just off the Belt Parkway in Brooklyn. Drivers, park your vehicles at the huge Toys-R-Us shopping center right next to the park.

Directions

0.0 **From the parking lot next to the park, head toward the bay and turn RIGHT along the water to pick up the bicycle path. Walk your bike past the playground, then resume riding after a speed bump. Follow the path for about four miles as it takes you along the Narrows and underneath the Verrazano-Narrows Bridge.**

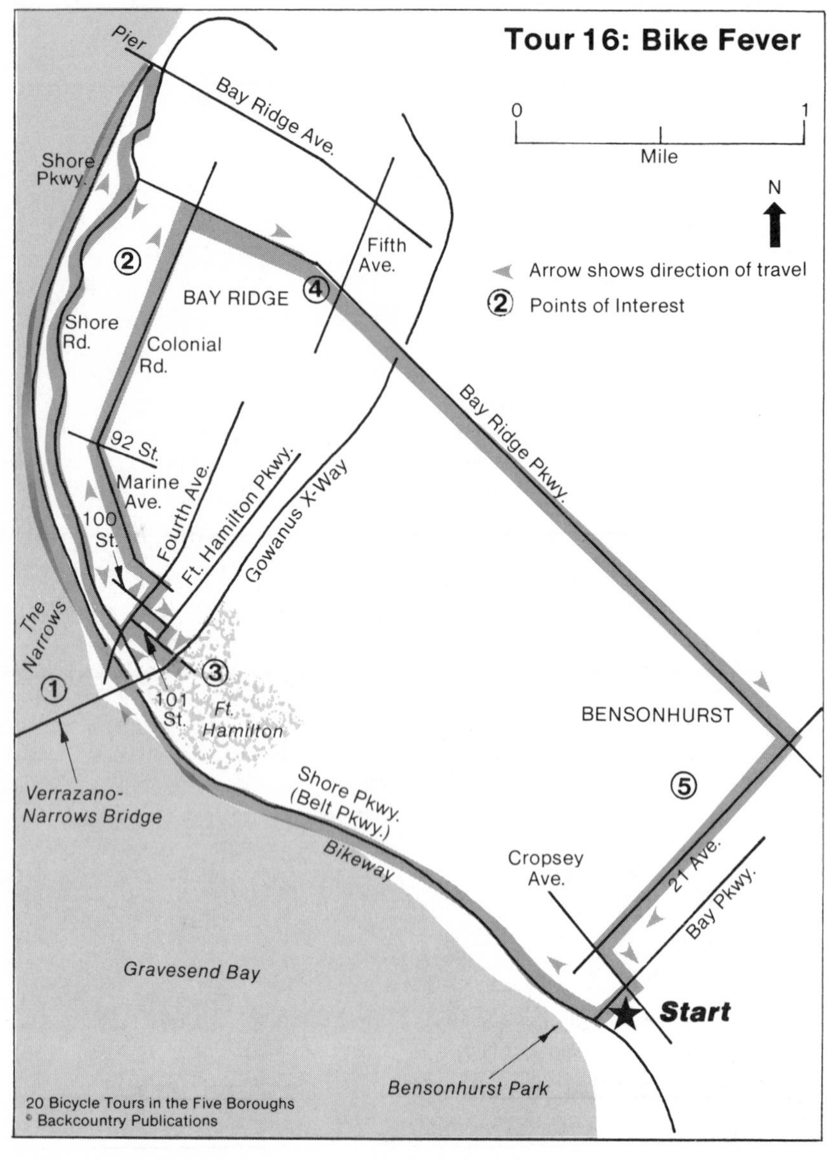

The most recent addition to the city's bevy of beautiful bridges, this span was completed in 1964, linking Bay Ridge, Brooklyn, with Fort Wadsworth on Staten Island. At 4,260 feet, the Verrazano-Narrows is the world's longest suspension bridge, surpassing the Golden Gate Bridge in San Francisco by sixty feet.

The promenade along the Narrows is one of the best-maintained and most popular bike routes in the city. It can get quite crowded on sunny weekend afternoons; you'll have to share the right-of-way with strollers, joggers, fishermen and other cyclists. (1)

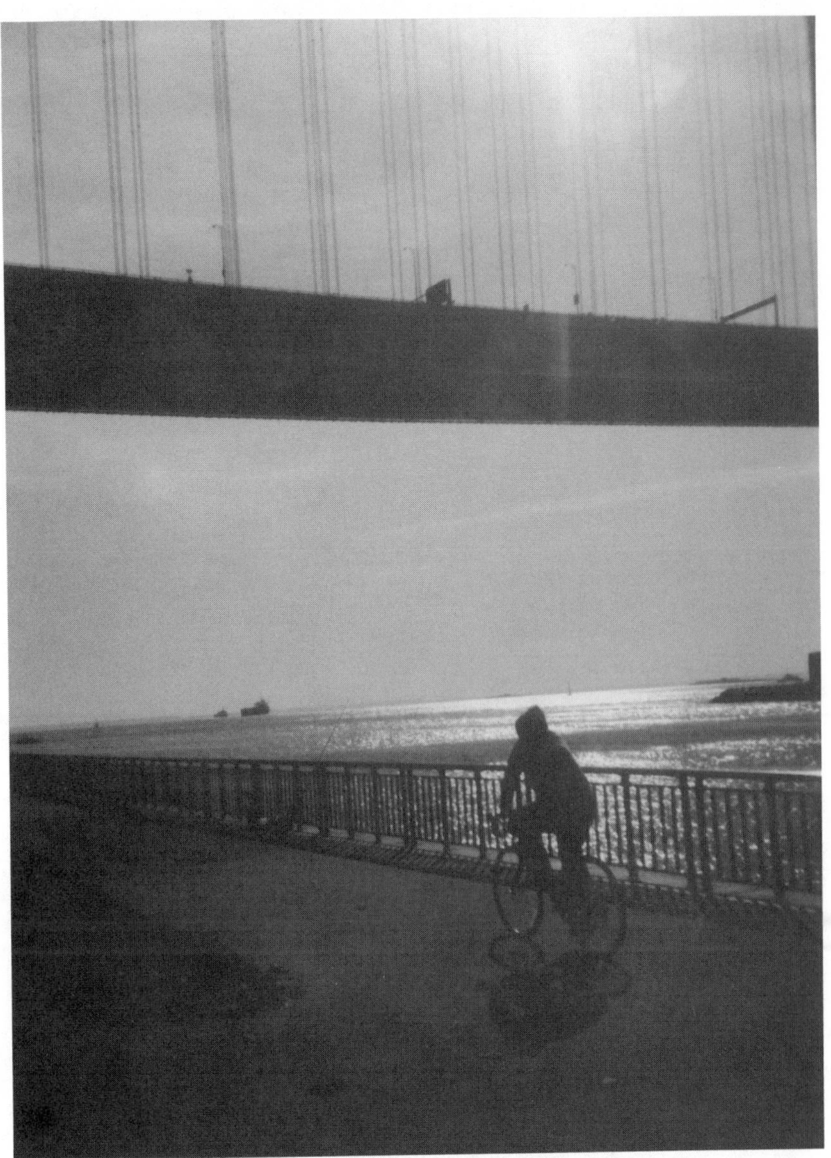

Shore Parkway bicycle path and Verrazano Bridge.

4.2 When you reach a large concrete fishing pier at the end of the promenade, turn RIGHT, onto Bay Ridge Avenue.

Before turning, stop to admire the view from the pier. On a clear day, the dazzling panorama takes in the Verrazano-Narrows Bridge, Staten Island, New York Harbor, the Lower Manhattan skyline, and even the distant Statue of Liberty.

4.3 Take the first RIGHT, at Shore Road.

Bay Ridge was once one of Brooklyn's most exclusive suburbs, and Shore Road was the borough's "scenic drive." The winding, rolling drive was once lined with the elaborate villas of wealthy landowners. Most of the mansions have since been replaced with blocks of luxury high-rise apartments. Lookout points from which to view the bay are situated at intervals along Shore Road. (2)

6.4 Turn LEFT at Fourth Avenue.

6.5 Take the second RIGHT, at 100th Street.

6.6 Turn RIGHT at the end, onto Fort Hamilton Parkway.

6.7 Turn LEFT at the end, into the entrance of Fort Hamilton, to visit the Harbor Defense Museum.

In August 1776 the Revolutionary War's largest battle, the Battle of Long Island, took place at this site. Seventy-five years later Fort Hamilton was constructed, facing Fort Wadsworth on Staten Island to protect the entrance to New York Harbor. Today, Fort Hamilton is New York City's only remaining active army post.

The Harbor Defense Museum is housed in a handsomely renovated flank battery. It offers changing exhibitions on military history and the coastal defense of New York, including a collection of cannons, guns, mines, and other military objects. The museum is open Monday, Thursday, and Friday from 1:00 p.m. to 4:00 p.m., on Saturday from 10:00 a.m. to 5:00 p.m., and on Sunday from 1:00 p.m. to 5:00 p.m. Admission is free. You must register with the guard at the entrance to the fort. (3)

Leaving Fort Hamilton the same way you entered, cross Fort Hamilton Parkway. Then take the first RIGHT, at Fourth Avenue.

7.0 Turn LEFT at Marine Avenue.

7.5 At 92nd Street, Marine Avenue bends to the right and becomes Colonial Road.

8.4 Turn RIGHT at Bay Ridge *Parkway* (not Bay Ridge *Avenue*).

Approaching the Bay Ridge commercial district, enter the Bay Ridge of Tony Manero and Company. Scenes from the film *Saturday Night Fever* were shot on location on local streets, at a neighbor-

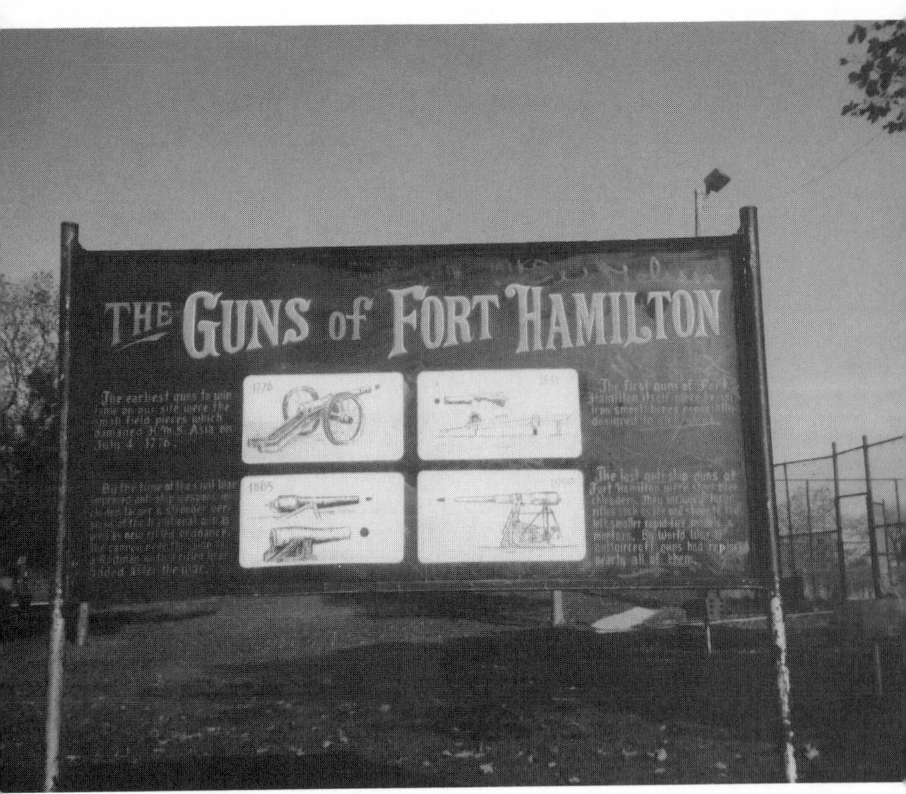

Harbor Defense Museum in Fort Hamilton.

hood pizza parlor on Third Avenue, and at the discotheque 2001, which is still operating on the outskirts of the neighborhood. Those who saw the film will never forget the fatal antics that took place on the rafters of the Verrazano Bridge.

Continue STRAIGHT on Bay Ridge Parkway.

Bay Ridge was once the site of a small but flourishing Scandinavian (mostly Norwegian) community that settled here because of the site's proximity to the harbor. For the most part, the community has disappeared. There remains, however, an eight-block stretch on Fifth Avenue off of Bay Ridge Parkway, where merchants offer such specialties as canned reindeer meatballs, lingonberry jam, and homemade crispbreads. To visit what is left of Scandinavian Bay Ridge, turn right at Fifth Avenue and look for stores with names like Fredricksen and Johannesens' Delicatessen, Leske's Danish Bakery, and the Scandinavian Gift Shoppe. The Scandinavian shops, most of which are located between 74th and 82nd Streets, are a bit hard to find among the ubiquitous pizza parlors and discount stores. (4)

Return to Bay Ridge Parkway and continue east.

11.4 Turn RIGHT at 21st Avenue, in Bensonhurst.

When the producers of *The Honeymooners* chose Bensonhurst as the program's locale, they did so because it was felt that Bensonhurst was the prototypical working-class Brooklyn neighborhood. The Kramdens' dingy sixth-floor walkup apartment was supposedly located at Chauncey Street. There is a Chauncey Street in Brooklyn, but it is in Bushwick, not Bensonhurst. The producers felt, however, that the name Bensonhurst was already recognizable to millions of Americans and so would be more acceptable to viewers all over the country as a setting for the series. The notoriety of the neighborhood has been used to advantage in other shows as well. Recently a character on the "Dallas" series was said to have come from Bensonhurst. Does the community live up to its reputation as the most quintessential of Brooklyn neighborhoods? With its haphazard mix of low-rise apartment buildings, rowhouses, single-family homes and mom-and-pop commercial establishments, I suppose it does. But so do many other neighborhoods throughout the borough.

12.3 Turn LEFT at Cropsey Avenue.

12.5 Turn RIGHT at Bay Parkway, back to the parking lot at Bensonhurst Park.

Bicycle Shops

Bay Ridge Bicycle World, 8916 Third Avenue (between 89th & 90th Sts.) (718-238-1118)

Dyker Bike Shop, 8310 13th Avenue, Bensonhurst (718-745-4494)

Phil's Fixit Shop, 2308 86th Street (one block from Bay Parkway), Bensonhurst (718-372-1013)

Shore-Belt Cycle Club, 29 Bay Ridge Avenue (near Shore Road), Bay Ridge (718-748-5077)

17
Ethnic New York

Distance: 12 miles
Terrain: flat
Traffic: heavy

All of New York is "ethnic" New York. Yet certain neighborhoods identify much more strongly with their ethnic origins than others. One of those is Manhattan's Lower East Side, which has been home to wave after wave of immigrants ever since the city was founded. The Lower East Side is the domain of Chinatown, Little Italy, and the Jewish landmarks of East Broadway and Grand Street. Just over the Williamsburg Bridge, in northern Brooklyn, are two more communities that are also among the most solidly ethnic in the city: Orthodox Jewish Williamsburg and Polish-Russian Greenpoint both bear the stamp of the ethnic groups that have long dominated the region. This thoroughly urban tour explores a bit of the Lower East Side, then follows the trail of immigration across the Williamsburg Bridge into northern Brooklyn.

Before deciding to embark on this tour, note the following conditions. First, the road conditions in northern Brooklyn and on the Williamsburg Bridge are among the worst in the city. Think twice before bringing a very delicate or expensive bike here. Second, in Brooklyn, the route passes through an area that is not among the city's showcases. Williamsburg and Greenpoint are safe neighborhoods, but—as is usually the case—the marginal area in between is a no-man's-land that may appear frightening to some people. Those people may feel more comfortable traveling with a companion.

The ride begins at Chatham Square, at the intersection of Bowery and East Broadway, in the heart of Chinatown. There are some private and municipal parking lots around, but be advised—this part of town is always jumping, even on Sundays, and parking is difficult.

Directions

0.0 From Chatham Square, head south on St. James Place for one block. On your left behind a black iron railing is a tiny cemetery that bears the remains of the first Jewish settlers of New Amsterdam (later New York). In 1654, after the Portuguese conquered Brazil, a group of Sephardic Jews was expelled from a South American port city.

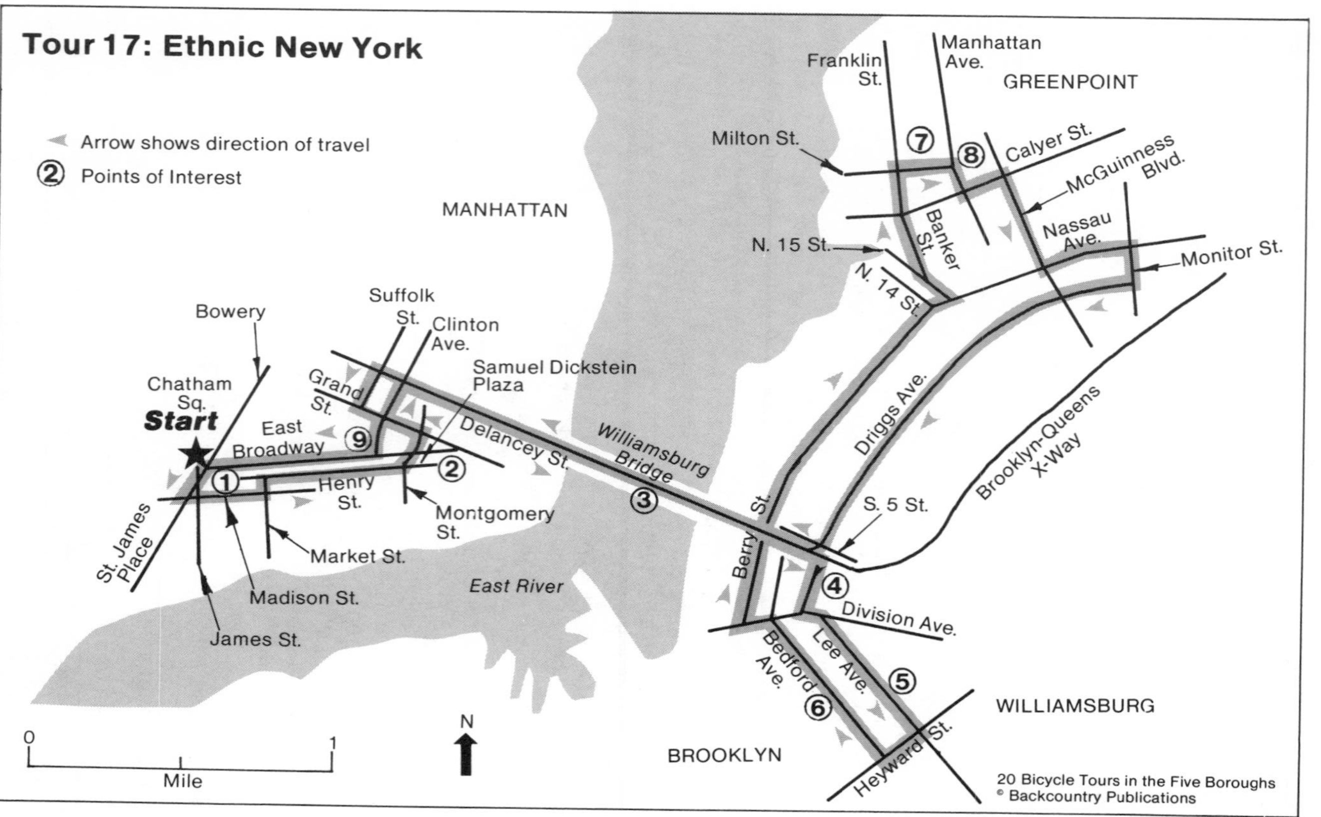

Tour 17: Ethnic New York
Arrow shows direction of travel
2 Points of Interest
MANHATTAN
GREENPOINT
WILLIAMSBURG
BROOKLYN
East River
Start
Chatham Sq.
Bowery
St. James Place
East Broadway
James St.
Madison St.
Market St.
Henry St.
Grand St.
Suffolk St.
Clinton Ave.
Montgomery St.
Samuel Dickstein Plaza
Delancey St.
Williamsburg Bridge
Berry St.
Bedford Ave.
Lee Ave.
Heyward St.
Division Ave.
S. 5 St.
Driggs Ave.
Brooklyn-Queens X-Way
Monitor St.
Nassau Ave.
McGuinness Blvd.
Calyer St.
Manhattan Ave.
Banker St.
Franklin St.
Milton St.
N. 15 St.
N. 14 St.
N
0
1
Mile
20 Bicycle Tours in the Five Boroughs
© Backcountry Publications

Twenty-three men, women, and children made their way to New York Harbor, only to be refused entry by the anti-Semitic governor, Peter Stuyvesant, who feared that the penniless refugees would be a burden to the colony. But many of the shareholders of the Dutch West India Company (which had founded the settlement of New Amsterdam) were Jewish and pressured the governor to let the Jews in. The landmark Spanish-Portuguese cemetery on St. James Place is said to be the oldest artifact on the island of Manhattan and the oldest Jewish relic in the United States. (1)

Take the first LEFT, at James Street.

0.1 Take the first LEFT, at Madison Street.

0.3 Turn LEFT at Market Street.

0.4 Turn RIGHT at Henry Street.

The "old-law" tenements, designed to house the masses of immigrants who came to New York City in the latter part of the 1800s, were notoriously overcrowded and unhealthy. Often ten people

Henry Street Settlement on the Lower East Side.

would share a single room with no natural light or ventilation. The Tenement House Reform Bill of 1901 outlawed the further construction of such buildings and required that all new residential buildings allow for direct natural lighting of every room and include separate toilet facilities for each apartment. Many old-law tenements are still standing on the Lower East Side.

1.0 Turn LEFT at Samuel Dickstein Plaza (opposite Montgomery Street).

Just beyond the intersection, on Henry Street, stands a row of well-preserved red-brick Federal-style structures that housed one of the nation's original social agencies. As wave after wave of destitute immigrants crowded into the slums of the Lower East Side during the late nineteenth and early twentieth centuries, a nurse named Lillian Wald founded the Nurse's Settlement to provide medical care and other services for the community. Today, the Henry Street Settlement continues to operate as a nonprofit social service organization for the Lower East Side. (2)

1.1 Turn LEFT at Grand Street.

1.2 Turn RIGHT at Clinton Street.

1.3 Turn RIGHT at Delancey Street, onto the promenade at the center of the Williamsburg Bridge. Cross the bridge, which spans the East River.

Completed in 1903, this bridge was the major avenue by which some Lower East Side immigrants overflowed into Brooklyn. The wide pedestrian mall at the center of the bridge provided a link between the Jewish communities of the Lower East Side and Williamsburg, Brooklyn. Although the pedestrian ramp, which is suspended over the main thoroughfare, offers excellent views of the Manhattan and Brooklyn skylines, this is not an easy crossing for bicyclists. The promenade and the bridge as a whole are in such poor condition that the entire structure had to be closed during the spring of 1988, when inspectors found serious cracks and corrosion. There was speculation that this major East River crossing would have to be torn down and replaced. After many weeks of traffic nightmares, however, the bridge was pronounced "reparable" and reopened to traffic. (3)

2.7 Turn RIGHT at the foot of the bridge, onto Driggs Avenue.

This is not a pretty sight as you come off the bridge. There are, however, two important Brooklyn landmarks at the foot of the bridge. The Williamsburg Savings Bank, at the corner of Driggs Avenue and Broadway, is noted for its majestic dome and monumental entrance. And across the street from the bank, the Peter Luger Steakhouse has been a New York culinary tradition since 1876. (4)

Hebrew storefront in Williamsburg.

2.9 Turn LEFT at Division Avenue. Then bear RIGHT immediately, onto Lee Avenue.

Lee Avenue is the main shopping street in this community of ultra-Orthodox Hasidic Jews. Signs in Hebrew and Yiddish advertise everything from traditional religious garments to Kosher pizza. If you've chosen to take this tour on a Saturday, you will enjoy streets almost totally devoid of traffic, since the members of this sect are strictly forbidden to perform any work or to drive cars on the Jewish Sabbath. (5)

3.5 Turn RIGHT at Heyward Street.

3.6 Take the first RIGHT, at Bedford Avenue.

More Jewish institutions, schools, and synagogues occupy the once-elegant mansions along this avenue. Many of these "mansions" are architectural jewels and were built before the opening of the Williamsburg Bridge. As you continue north, however, the neighborhood becomes increasingly desolate. Many of the buildings are being razed or renovated by the Hasidic community. (6)

4.2 Turn LEFT at Division Avenue.

4.3 Take the first RIGHT, at Berry Avenue.

You'll probably want to leave this area behind as quickly as possible.

5.4 Berry Avenue curves to the right and becomes Nassau Avenue at North 14th Street.

5.5 Take the next LEFT, at North 15th Street. Then bear RIGHT immediately onto Banker Street.

5.9 Banker Street merges into Franklin Street just past Calyer Street.

6.0 Turn RIGHT at Milton Street.

The community of Greenpoint originated as a major ship-building center at the turn of the century. Several areas in the neighborhood (including this street) were designated Historic Districts and contain homes built by the wealthy shipyard tycoons of that era. (7)

6.2 Turn RIGHT at the end, onto Manhattan Avenue.

Greenpoint is predominantly Polish in its ethnic makeup. On Manhattan Avenue, the commercial center, you'll find such ethnic landmarks as the Chopin Theatre and the Polonaise Terrace Catering Hall, in addition to numerous Polish restaurants, groceries, and bakeries. In some of the neighborhood churches, the masses and hymns are performed in Polish. (8)

6.3 Turn LEFT at Calyer Street.

6.5 Turn RIGHT at McGuiness Boulevard.

6.8 Turn LEFT at Nassau Avenue.

7.1 Turn RIGHT at Monitor Street, along the edge of McGoldrick Park.

7.3 Turn RIGHT at Driggs Avenue.

8.8 Turn RIGHT, onto the pedestrian mall of the Williamsburg Bridge, just past South 5th Street. Cross the bridge.

10.1 Coming off the bridge in Manhattan, turn LEFT at Suffolk Street.

10.3 **Turn LEFT at Grand Street.**

10.5 **Turn RIGHT at East Broadway, which leads you back to Chatham Square.**

The ethnic group that left the strongest imprint on the Lower East Side was the Eastern European Jewish immigrants who arrived around the turn of the century. East Broadway is a treasure trove of relics from that era. In addition to the row of storefront synagogues, called *shteeblech,* and the old-law tenements that line the street, there are two distinguished Historic Landmarks on East Broadway. The Seward Park branch of the New York Public Library, at 192 East Broadway (at Jefferson Street), houses one of the largest collections of Jewish literature and Yiddish books in the nation. Across the street from the library, at number 175, is the Jewish Daily Forward Building, which was the headquarters of a highly influential Yiddish daily newspaper and the cultural center of the immigrant community. (9)

Bicycle Shops

Frank's Bike Shop, 553 Grand Street (near Franklin Delano Roosevelt Drive), Lower East Side (212-553-6332)

Hooper Street Garage, 396 Hooper Street, Williamsburg (718-486-8456)

18

Staten Island: Before the Bridge

Distance: 16 miles
Terrain: hilly
Traffic: light

The completion of the Verrazano-Narrows Bridge in 1964 changed the face of Staten Island. It brought runaway development and hundreds of thousands of newcomers to New York City's "last frontier." But there *was* a Staten Island before the bridge. Old established communities, mostly in the borough's northern section, flourished long before the Verrazano was built. St. George, New Brighton, and Port Richmond were early settlements that grew up around the ferry terminus and the island's waterfront industry. Sailors' Snug Harbor, a former haven for retired seamen and now the borough's most celebrated historic landmark, is another relic of that maritime heritage. This tour takes in some of the portions of the island where time has stood still. The ride will test your stamina on hills as steep as San Francisco's, with correspondingly breathtaking views of New York Harbor and the Atlantic Ocean.

The trip begins with a long, stiff climb to the top of Grymes Hill, followed by an equally strenuous ascent up Emerson Hill. Don't get discouraged—you'll be rewarded with some memorable views and a long, easy coast back down to sea level. And afterward the route levels out somewhat for the remainder of the tour. The tour departs from the Staten Island Ferry terminal in St. George; you might want to begin the day with a trip over from Manhattan on the ferry. It's 25¢ for a round trip for cyclists.

Directions

0.0 Leaving the ferry terminal, turn LEFT onto Bay Street.

St. George, Staten Island's civic center, looks especially intriguing from the deck of the approaching ferryboat. Wooded hills, church spires, and towers rise behind the Greek Revival facades of the official buildings. Directly across from the terminal is Borough Hall, which is flanked by the Family and County Courthouses. (1)

0.4 Turn RIGHT at Victory Boulevard, uphill for about a mile.

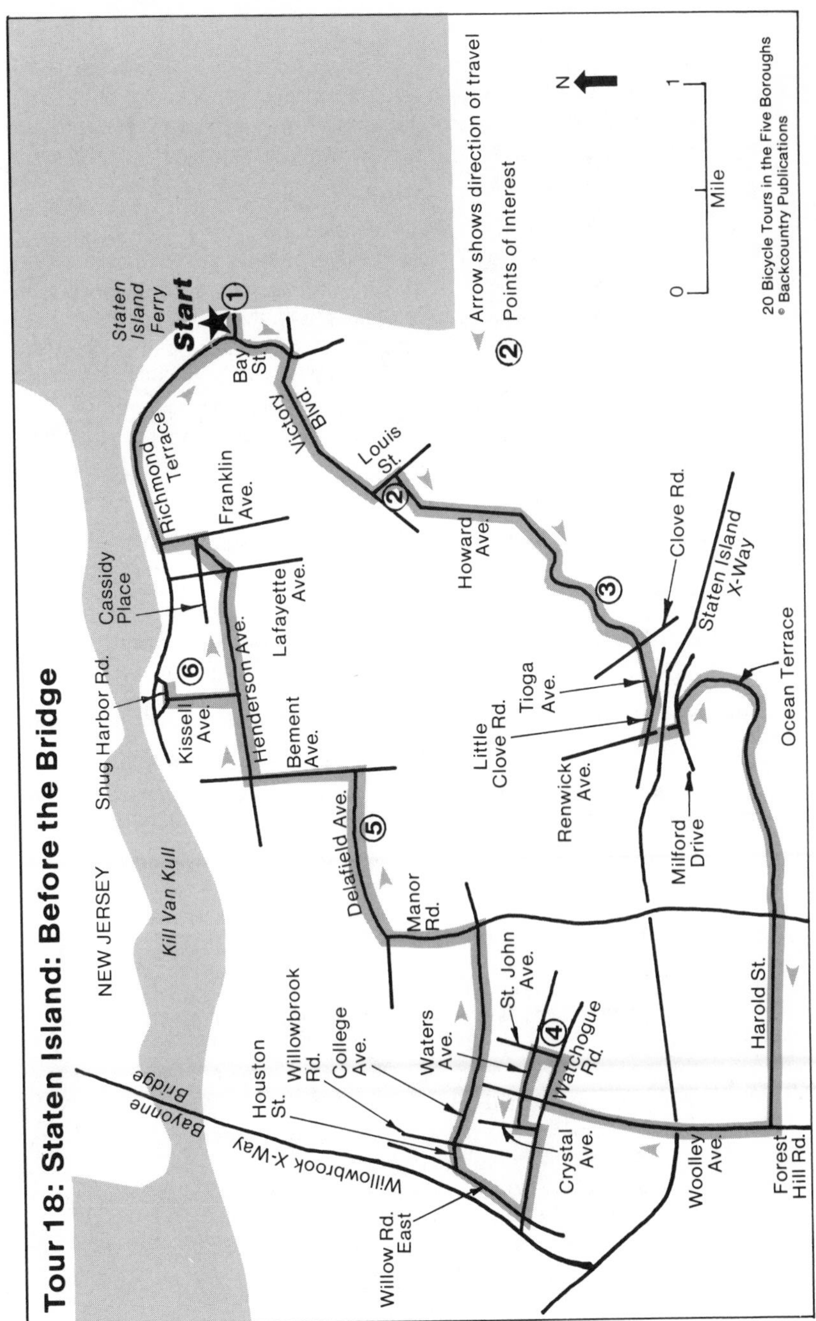
Tour 18: Staten Island: Before the Bridge
Staten Island Ferry
Start
Bay St.
Victory Blvd.
Louis St.
Richmond Terrace
Franklin Ave.
Cassidy Place
Lafayette Ave.
Henderson Ave.
Snug Harbor Rd.
Kissell Ave.
Bement Ave.
NEW JERSEY
Kill Van Kull
Delafield Ave.
Manor Rd.
Howard Ave.
Clove Rd.
Staten Island X-Way
Tioga Ave.
Little Clove Rd.
Renwick Ave.
Milford Drive
Ocean Terrace
Harold St.
St. John Ave.
Watchogue Rd.
Waters Ave.
College Ave.
Willowbrook Rd.
Houston St.
Bayonne Bridge
Willowbrook X-Way
Willow Rd. East
Crystal Ave.
Woolley Ave.
Forest Hill Rd.
Arrow shows direction of travel
Points of Interest
N
0
1
Mile
20 Bicycle Tours in the Five Boroughs
© Backcountry Publications

1.4 Turn LEFT at Louis Street, steeply uphill.

On your right as you turn onto Louis Street is a fine example of the city's so-called vest-pocket parks. Beautifully landscaped Hero Park was donated by Dr. and Mrs. Louis Dreyfus to commemorate the victims of World War I. A memorial plaque appears at the lower entrance to the park. (2)

1.6 Take the first RIGHT at Howard Avenue.

Howard Avenue used to be called Serpentine Road. Some say the name is derived from a type of rock, called serpentinite, that is abundant in the area, but I prefer to think the zigzag course of the road is responsible. The road makes several sharp turns, so pay attention to stay on Howard Avenue. At the crest of the hill, the avenue winds past Wagner College on your left. Founded in 1883 as an Augustinian academy, the college today is nonsectarian and coed. The campus is a good place to enjoy some glorious views of New York Bay and the Verrazano-Narrows Bridge to the east. (3)

3.2 Howard Avenue becomes Tioga Street as you cross Clove Road at the bottom of the hill. Tioga Street merges into Little Clove Road along the expressway.

3.6 Turn LEFT at Renwick Avenue, underneath the expressway.

3.7 Turn LEFT at the end, onto Milford Drive, then bear RIGHT immediately onto unmarked Ocean Terrace, past the campus of Staten Island Community College on your right.

5.3 Ocean Terrace becomes Harold Street as you cross Manor Road at the bottom of the hill.

6.4 Turn RIGHT at the end of Harold Street, onto Forest Hill Road. Forest Hill Road becomes Woolley Avenue.

7.5 Turn RIGHT at Watchogue Road.

7.7 Turn LEFT at St. John Avenue.

The community of Westerleigh is one of the best-preserved examples of Staten Island as it looked "before the bridge." The area was originally known as Prohibition Park; a community of teetotalers was established there in 1898 as a refuge for prohibitionists around the country. Streets in the neighborhood were named after "dry" states —Maine, Ohio, Virginia—or after Prohibition Party presidential candidates—Bidwell, Woolley, Fiske. The early street names are still in place, but today's residents no longer proclaim their sobriety. (4)

7.8 Turn LEFT at Waters Avenue.

8.2 Turn LEFT at the end, onto Crystal Avenue.

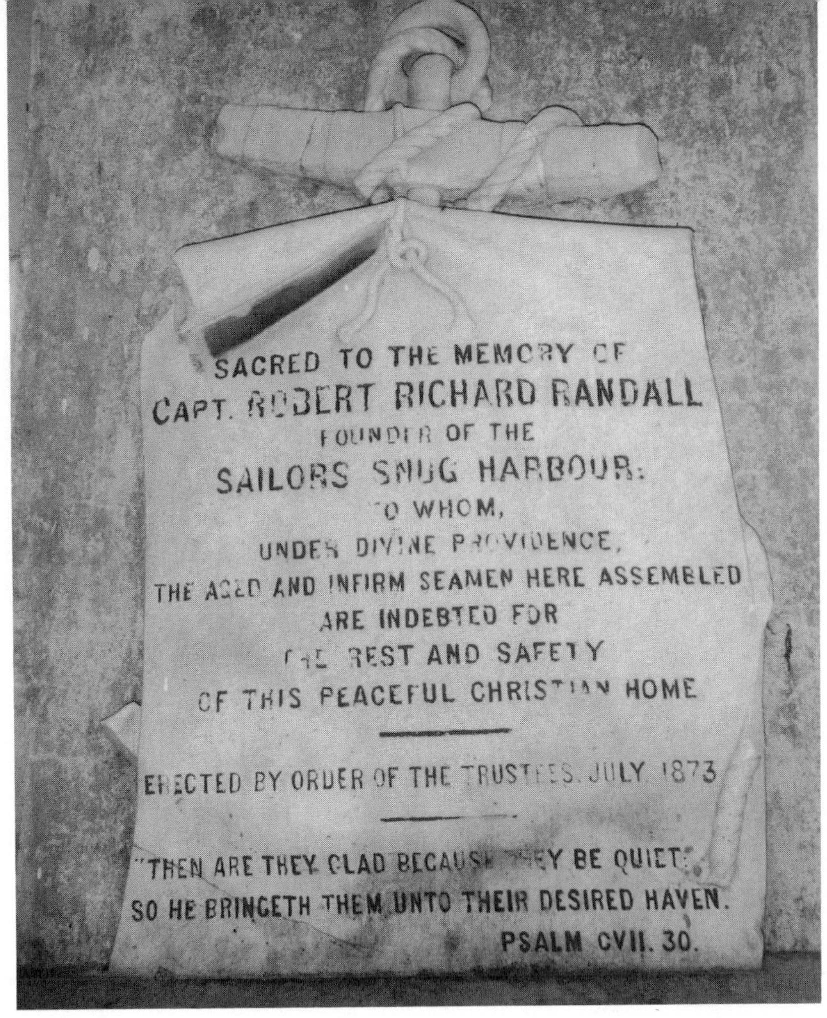

Sailor's Snug Harbor.

8.3 Take the first RIGHT, back onto Watchogue Road.

8.8 Turn RIGHT at Willow Road East, along the highway.

9.2 Bear RIGHT at Houston Street, which becomes College Avenue as you cross Willowbrook Road.

10.2 Turn LEFT at Manor Road.

10.7 Turn RIGHT at the end, onto Delafield Avenue.

On your right at 752 Delafield Avenue is the landmark Scotts-Edwards House, a Dutch colonial farmhouse built in 1730. (5)

11.5 Turn LEFT at the end, onto Bement Avenue.

11.9 Turn RIGHT at Henderson Avenue.

12.4 Turn LEFT at Kissel Avenue.

12.7 Turn RIGHT at the end, onto Snug Harbor Road; then take the first RIGHT into the Sailors' Snug Harbor Culture Center.

This former haven for retired seamen (called "Snugs") was purchased by the city in 1976 in an effort to save its rich complex of early-twentieth-century buildings from demolition. The star attraction of the site is the row of "Greek temples" overlooking the front lawn and the Kill Van Kull. The are among the finest examples of this architectural style in the country. Sixty acres of rolling parkland behind the temples encompass a wealth of hidden sculptures, fountains, grottoes, gardens, ponds, and cottages. The entire complex has been given landmark status and is undergoing restoration. The grounds are currently home to an array of cultural institutions, including the Staten Island Botanical Garden, the Children's Museum, and the Institute of Arts and Sciences. These organizations offer exhibitions of sculpture, painting, and photography, as well as theatrical and musical events. Bike racks, maps, and information are available at the visitor center near the West Gate. (6)

Leaving the Snug Harbor Culture Center the same way you entered, turn LEFT onto Snug Harbor Road, then take the first LEFT at Kissel Avenue.

13.4 Turn LEFT, back onto Henderson Avenue, which merges into unmarked Cassidy Place after you cross Lafayette Avenue.

14.2 Turn LEFT at the end, onto Franklin Avenue.

14.4 Turn RIGHT at the end, onto Richmond Terrace, which will take you back to the ferry terminal.

Bicycle Shops

Seriously Cycles, 500 Henderson Street, West New Brighton (718-816-8611)
Lombardi Bicycles, 440 Bay Street, Stapleton (718-447-9722)

19

Staten Island Greenbelt Tour

Distance: 19 miles
Terrain: hilly
Traffic: moderate

Less than an hour away from Times Square, near the heart of Staten Island, lies a U-shaped band of open space called the Greenbelt—nearly two thousand acres of undeveloped land that includes a wildlife refuge, a National Environmental Education Landmark, a historic cemetery, and portions of the Gateway National Recreation Area. Although endless tracts of new housing developments have marched right up to its borders, the pristine acreage within the Greenbelt itself remains intact, thanks to the efforts of conservationists and the New York City Parks Department. The result is a delightful patchwork of woods, wetlands, and meadows, interrupted by neighborhoods—some quaint and old-fashioned, others so new they are still under construction. Hikers can appreciate this natural area on a thirty-five-mile network of nature trails; cyclists can experience it on the lightly traveled roads that encircle and cross its spaces.

This is not an easy ride. A couple of steep hills (including formidable Todt Hill), some narrow roads with no shoulders, and fast-moving traffic make the going rough in spots. But the rewards of exploring this uniquely scenic region make the trip well worth the effort. Begin the tour at the entrance to the huge Staten Island Mall, located inside the U of the Greenbelt at Richmond Avenue and Platinum Avenue. You can get there by taking the Staten Island Expressway to Richmond Avenue (not Richmond Road), then heading south for about two miles to the mall.

Directions

0.0 Head up Platinum Avenue.

0.5 Turn LEFT at the end, onto Forest Hill Road.

The wooded area on your right is a part of La Tourette Park, the largest single tract within the Greenbelt. It includes 580 acres of woodland and marsh along a chain of hills, a public golf course, and the ninety-four-acre Richmondtown Restoration, an eighteenth-century village restored by the Staten Island Historical Society. (1)

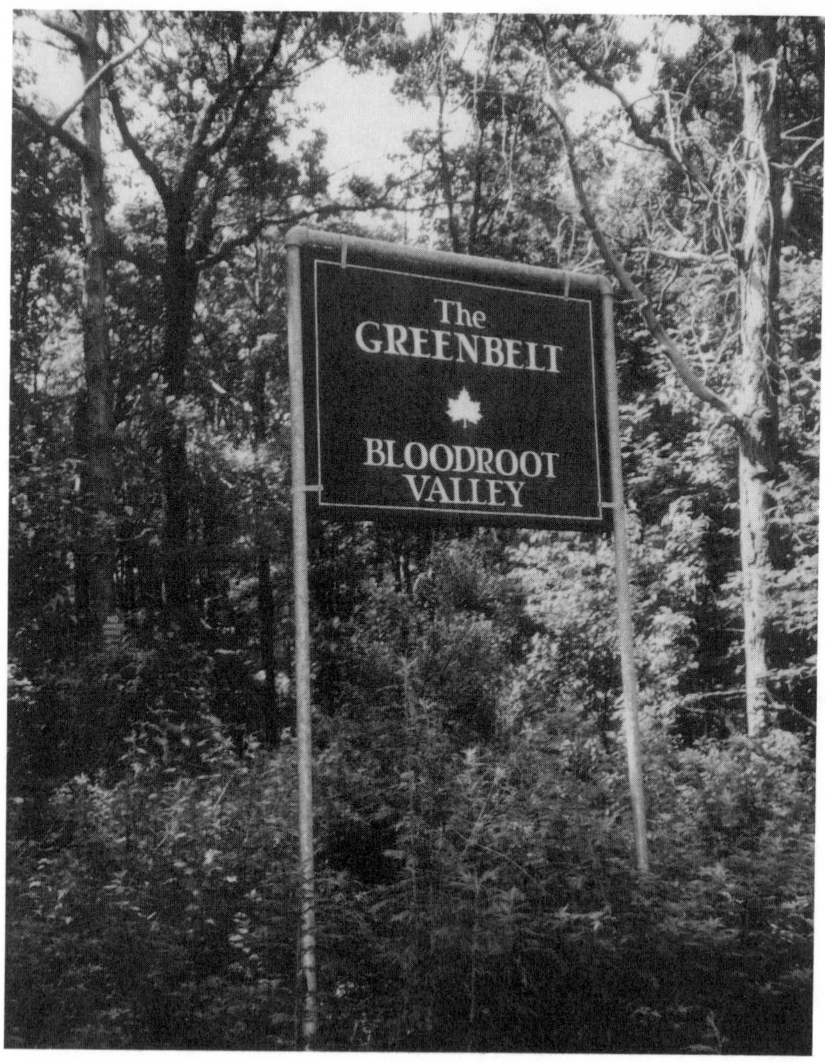

Along the Greenbelt.

1.1 **Cross Richmond Hill Road at the top of the hill and continue STRAIGHT, northeast on Forest Hill Road.**

Before you continue, you might want to detour a few blocks to the *left* on Richmond Hill Road. At number 435 is a gray clapboard farmhouse that, together with its neighboring red barn and outbuildings, has been restored by the Staten Island Historical Society as a farm of the 1830s. There is a working farm on the premises, which comes as a surprise in this newly constructed neighborhood of cookie-cutter housing developments. (2)

Returning to Forest Hill Road, you might want to make another detour, this time to the *right* on Richmond Hill Road. About a half-

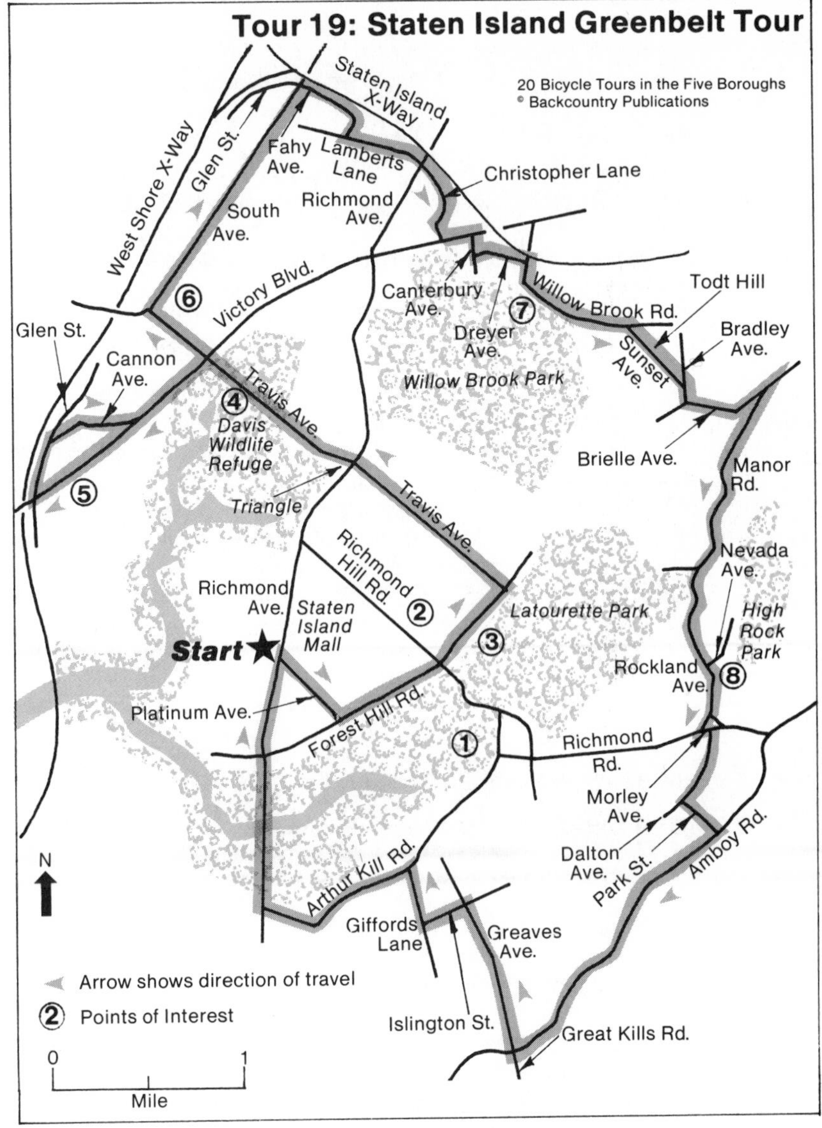

mile down the road on your left, set well back from the road, is a landmark 1836 Greek Revival mansion that now houses the La Tourette Park Clubhouse. It was once occupied by David La Tourette, who farmed the land now occupied by the park. (3)

Return to Forest Hill Road and continue northeast.

1.5 Turn LEFT at Travis Avenue, opposite the golf course, for a mile-long downhill coast.

2.5 At the bottom of the hill, cross Richmond Avenue. Pick up Travis Avenue again just beyond a triangle with a little office building on your left.

The wooded area on your left as you continue on Travis Avenue is the William T. Davis Wildlife Refuge, 260 acres of marshes, wet woodlands, freshwater swamps, and open meadows. Established in 1933, the Davis Refuge was the first such sanctuary in New York City. Wading birds like the great blue heron and the common egret are found here, along with hundreds of other species of wildlife. A 1.5-mile nature trail winds through eighty acres of the refuge, beginning at an opening on your left, just off Travis Avenue, on the west side of Richmond Avenue. (4)

3.5 Turn LEFT at the next traffic light, onto Victory Boulevard.

In contrast to the new housing developments that are covering more and more of western Staten Island, the quaint, secluded community of Travis evokes memories of the borough's past. The village changed its name to Linoleumville in 1873, when the American Linoleum Company established a plant here. But the company failed during the Great Depression, and the plant closed in 1931. A few years later, the disappointed village resumed its original name of Travis. (5)

4.5 Turn RIGHT at Glen Street, then stay to the right to avoid the expressway.

4.8 Turn RIGHT at the end, onto Cannon Avenue (*not* onto Parish Avenue).

5.1 Turn LEFT at the end, onto Victory Boulevard.

5.6 Turn LEFT at the traffic light, back onto Travis Avenue.

6.0 Turn RIGHT at the end, onto South Avenue, past the Teleport on your right.

Staten Island boasts the world's first space satellite communications center, the Teleport, on its northwestern shore. The office park surrounding the Teleport is interconnected to a regional fibre-optic cable network and provides state-of-the-art housing for businesses requiring instantaneous information from around the world. (6)

The Teleport, space satellite communications center.

7.5 Just *before* you reach the elevated Staten Island Expressway, turn RIGHT at unmarked Fahy Street (opposite Glen Street), which is also the expressway service road. It curves to the right.

8.0 Turn LEFT at Lamberts Lane. It becomes Christopher Lane as you cross Richmond Avenue.

8.8 **Turn LEFT at the end, onto Victory Boulevard.**

8.9 **Take the second RIGHT at Canterbury Avenue.**

9.0 **Turn LEFT at the end, onto Dreyer Avenue.**

9.3 **Turn RIGHT at the end, onto Willowbrook Road, past Willowbrook Park on your right.**

Barely visible through the foliage are some of the remains of the infamous Willowbrook State School, an institution for retarded children that closed in the 1970s amid shocking allegations of scandal and abuse. (7)

10.0 **Bear RIGHT at Sunset Avenue, uphill.**

This is the beginning of a long, strenuous climb up the west face of Todt Hill. At 410 feet, Todt Hill is the highest tidewater elevation on the Atlantic seaboard south of Mt. Desert Island in Maine.

10.5 **Turn RIGHT at Bradley Avenue.**

10.6 **Turn LEFT at Brielle Avenue.**

11.0 **Take the first RIGHT at Manor Road, downhill.**

The grooved pavement on this winding, downhill run makes for an uncomfortable ride. Be careful.

12.4 **Turn LEFT at the traffic light, onto Rockland Road, past High Rock Park on your left.**

This ninety-four-acre tract of hardwood forest has been designated a National Environmental Education Landmark because of its outstanding environment and programs. The preserve includes five woodland trails, a feel-touch-smell garden for the blind, and an environmental education research library with two thousand volumes housed in a historic stone cottage. Access to the preserve is via Nevada Avenue, about a quarter-mile down Rockland Avenue on the left. But be advised that you will have to climb steeply to reach the entrance, which is at the crest of a hill 225 feet above sea level. (8)

13.0 **Take a sharp LEFT at Morley Avenue, just before Rockland Avenue becomes Richmond Road and curves to the right.**

13.1 **Take the first RIGHT at Dalton Avenue.**

13.4 **Turn LEFT at the end, onto Park Street.**

13.6 **Turn RIGHT at the end, onto Amboy Road.**

15.4 **Turn RIGHT at Greaves Avenue, opposite Great Kills Road.**

16.2 **Turn LEFT at the end, onto Islington Street.**

16.4 **Turn RIGHT at Giffords Lane.**

16.6 Turn LEFT at the end, onto Arthur Kill Road.

17.5 Turn RIGHT at Richmond Avenue. Head STRAIGHT back to Platinum Avenue and the mall at 18.7 miles.

Use the sidewalk-bikeway along Richmond Avenue. It's much safer, and you'll rarely meet a pedestrian. To your right are the wetlands of La Tourette Park.

Bicycle Shops

Roald Bike Shop, 1434 Richmond Road (about two miles east of Amboy Road), Dongan Hills (718-351-7575)

20

Tottenville Triangle

Distance: 24 miles
Terrain: rolling
Traffic: light

The southern tip of Staten Island, where the Arthur Kill meets Raritan Bay, was originally called Billopps Point. It was named after an English sea captain who supposedly sailed around the island in less than twenty-four hours, thereby winning it away from New Jersey for inclusion within New York State. Billopp's seventeenth-century home still stands on a bluff overlooking the confluence, but the fishing village that grew up around the site has long since changed its name to Tottenville, after another prominent Staten Island family. Nowhere in the five boroughs is remoteness from the city's center more deeply felt than in this sleepy corner of Richmond, where old-fashioned Victorian homes on shaded streets still outnumber tract houses and mini-malls. The historic Billopp House and the secluded charm of Tottenville are among the many attractions to be savored on this tour of the triangular southern portion of the borough. A former lighthouse turned orphanage, a state wildlife preserve, and a couple of ancient burial grounds with tombstones bearing the names of the area's earliest settlers are other milestones that turn up along the route.

And here's some good news for cyclists: This portion of the borough lies on the coastal plain beyond the chain of steep hills that form the island's "backbone," so the terrain is much flatter here than elsewhere on the island. There are some ups and downs, but nothing a moderately conditioned biker can't handle. Begin the ride at the Staten Island Mall, located on Richmond *Avenue* (not Richmond *Road*), between Richmond Hill Road and Platinum Avenue, in the New Springville section.

Directions

0.0 Leaving the mall, turn LEFT onto Richmond Avenue.
Traffic is fast and aggressive along this stretch. Also, watch out for the closely spaced storm drains along the curb.

1.1 Bear RIGHT at the first opportunity, onto Drumgoole Road West.

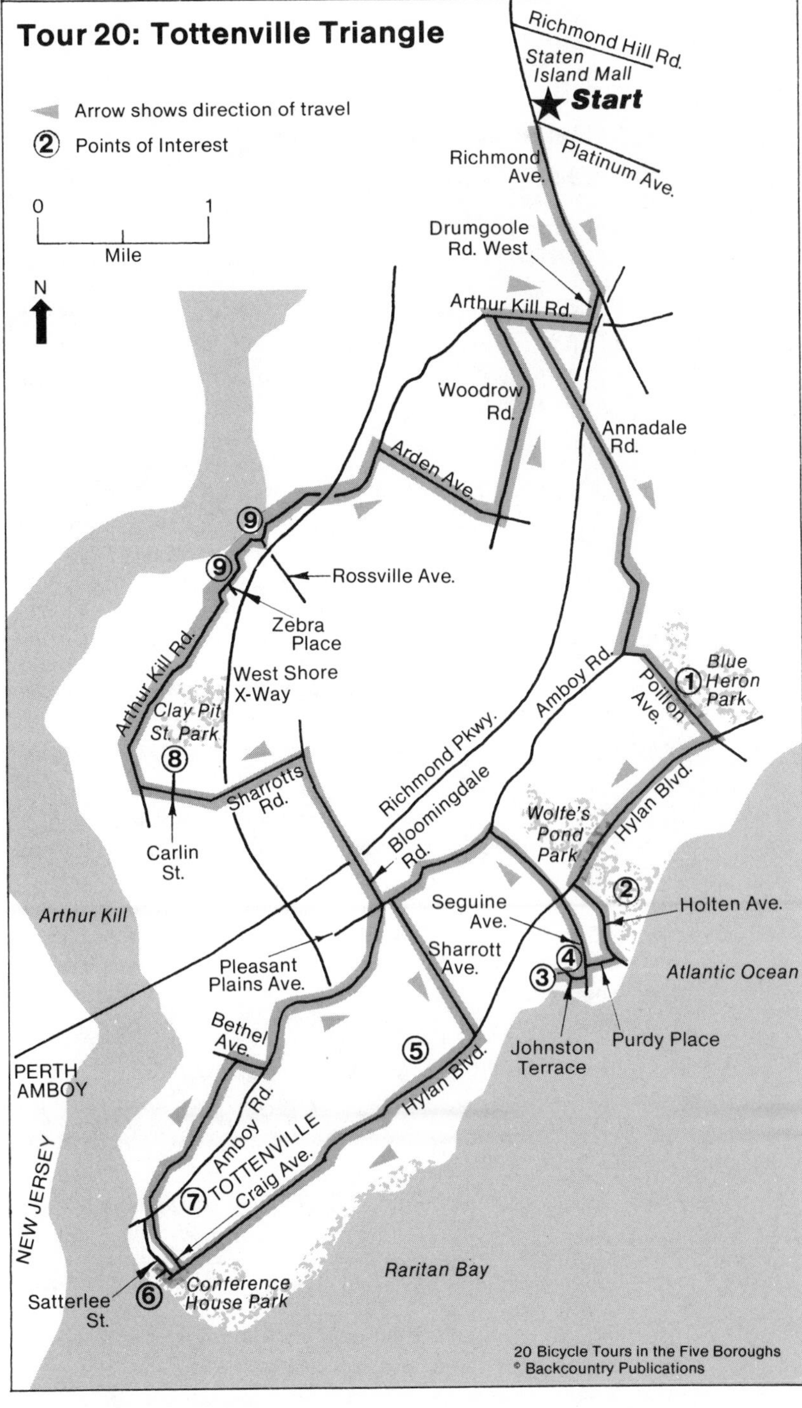

Tour 20: Tottenville Triangle
Arrow shows direction of travel
② Points of Interest
0
1
Mile
N
Richmond Hill Rd.
Staten Island Mall
Start
Platinum Ave.
Richmond Ave.
Drumgoole Rd. West
Arthur Kill Rd.
Woodrow Rd.
Annadale Rd.
Arden Ave.
9
9
Rossville Ave.
Zebra Place
West Shore X-Way
Arthur Kill Rd.
Clay Pit St. Park
8
Carlin St.
Sharrotts Rd.
Richmond Pkwy.
Amboy Rd.
Poillon Ave.
1
Blue Heron Park
Hylan Blvd.
Wolfe's Pond Park
Bloomingdale Rd.
2
Holten Ave.
Seguine Ave.
4
3
Sharrott Ave.
Atlantic Ocean
Arthur Kill
Pleasant Plains Ave.
Johnston Terrace
Purdy Place
Bethel Ave.
5
Hylan Blvd.
PERTH AMBOY
Amboy Rd.
TOTTENVILLE
Craig Ave.
7
NEW JERSEY
6
Satterlee St.
Conference House Park
Raritan Bay
20 Bicycle Tours in the Five Boroughs
© Backcountry Publications

1.3 **Take the first RIGHT, at Arthur Kill Road.**

1.6 **Turn LEFT at Annadale Road.**

3.6 **Turn LEFT at Amboy Road.**

3.7 **Take the first RIGHT, at Poillon Avenue.**

The wooded tracts on either side of the avenue belong to Blue Heron Park, a designated State Freshwater Wetland and a recent addition to the city park system. The park was named after the majestic wading birds that frequent its ponds and marshes. It is not at all unusual to spot one of the graceful gray or pale blue creatures fishing in the swamp just off Poillon Avenue. (1)

4.4 **Turn RIGHT at Hylan Boulevard.**

5.6 **Turn LEFT at Holton Avenue, at the far corner of Wolfe's Pond Park.**

Wolfe's Pond Park, on your left, encompasses 224 acres of both developed parkland and untouched natural woodland. Coming up on your left is Wolfe's Pond, a lovely freshwater "lake" favored by birdwatchers. The park extends south to the Atlantic coastline, where the beach has been developed for public swimming. (2)

6.1 **Turn RIGHT at Purdy Place, two blocks past the entrance to Wolfe's Pond. The street sign may be obscured by foliage.**

6.2 **Turn LEFT at the end, onto Seguine Avenue. Then take the first RIGHT, at Johnston Terrace, and proceed to the dead end.**

To the left off the dead end is a cluster of birdhouses that are home to the only colony of purple martins in New York City. The purple martin is a member of the swallow family that is ordinarily not found in urban areas—it prefers to nest in wide-open spaces. But the species is strongly attracted to the type of multichambered birdhouse seen here, and the colony has occupied this site for many years. The birds are thought to nest in colonies in order to deter predators and to share "information" about food sources. (3)

6.3 **Retrace your path to Seguine Avenue, and turn LEFT.**

To your left off Seguine Avenue, on a hill overlooking the marina, is the Seguine Mansion, a grand southern-plantation-style manor dating back to 1840. (4)

6.9 **Cross Hylan Boulevard and continue STRAIGHT on Seguine Avenue.**

7.4 **Turn LEFT at Amboy Road.**

The community of Princess Bay, like so many others in this part of Staten Island, had its origins as a fishing village, harvesting the once-famous oysters from Prince's Bay. Those oysters were carried, and designated by name, in the city's best restaurants.

8.2 Turn LEFT at Sharrott Avenue.

9.0 Turn RIGHT at Hylan Boulevard.

The rolling open spaces on either side of the boulevard belong to the 650-acre estate of the Mount Loretto Home for Children. The home, administered by the Mission of the Immaculate Virgin, is a haven for about a thousand orphans and children from broken homes. It was founded in 1870 by Father John C. Drumgoole. Coming up on the left, at the top of a low hill, is the former Prince's Bay Lighthouse, which now serves as the residence and dining hall for the priests who care for the children. The lighthouse beacon has been replaced by a statue of the Virgin Mary. The building is not open to the public. (5)

Continue STRAIGHT on Hylan Boulevard, following the signs to Conference House Park.

11.3 Turn RIGHT at the end of Hylan Boulevard, onto Satterlee Street. Then take the first LEFT, into the gravel driveway of the Billopp/Conference House.

The fieldstone manor house at the head of the driveway was built in 1680 by the aforementioned naval captain, Christopher Billopp, who allegedly won Staten Island away from New Jersey by sailing around the island in less than twenty-four hours. More important, the house was the site of a Revolutionary War conference that helped determine the course of American history. In 1776 the Battle of Long Island had taken place, giving control of New York to the British. On September 11, Lord Howe, the British commander, summoned the Americans to a meeting in which he offered amnesty to all American rebels who would lay down their arms and return to British allegiance. But Ben Franklin, John Adams, and Edmund Rutledge, representing the rebels, refused to surrender—and the rest is history. For more information and a tour of the manor, which is authentically furnished with mideighteenth-century pieces, you may visit the house Tuesday through Sunday from 1:00 p.m. to 5:00 p.m. Admission is free on Tuesday and Thursday. (6)

The house is surrounded by the rolling green lawns of Conference House Park, which slopes down to the Arthur Kill for a refreshing view of passing boats and Perth Amboy across the water in New Jersey.

Leaving the Conference House, turn RIGHT at Satterlee Street and go back to Hylan Boulevard.

11.4 Turn LEFT at Hylan, then take the first LEFT, at Craig Avenue.

11.8 Cross Amboy Road and continue STRAIGHT on Craig Avenue.

It is said that many Staten Islanders identify more closely with their

Historic Billopp/Conference House at the southern tip of Staten Island.

western neighbor, the state of New Jersey, than with the City of New York. A ride through Tottenville should help to explain this attitude. Not only is it the New York City community farthest from midtown Manhattan, but it is also the southernmost town in New York State. With the aura of a sleepy New Jersey resort town, Tottenville's side streets are lined with old-fashioned Victorian homes; some have wraparound porches, weatherbeaten shingles, and spired roofs. The commercial strip on Main Street is particularly evocative of another era. (7)

12.8 **Turn RIGHT at the end of Craig Avenue, onto Bethel Avenue.**

13.0 **Take the first LEFT, at Amboy Road.**

14.4 **At Pleasant Plains Avenue, Amboy Road bends sharply to the right. Do *not* follow Amboy Road to the right, but continue STRAIGHT across Pleasant Plains Avenue, onto Bloomingdale Road, going uphill.**

Soon the road narrows, and the absence of shoulders makes this an uncomfortable stretch.

15.4 **Turn LEFT at Sharrotts Road. Be prepared for a quarter-mile stretch of very bumpy road.**

16.2 **Turn RIGHT at Carlin Street to visit the Clay Pit Pond State Preserve.**

A young man looking for lizard specimens was responsible for the "discovery" of this unique wilderness on the western shore of Staten Island. The collector had searched the entire city without success; than he found a wealth of reptiles and amphibians here, in an area of abandoned clay mines (pits) that were filled with water, creating freshwater ponds of various sizes surrounded by pristine woodland. The 260-acre preserve, often compared to the New Jersey Pine Barrens, is noted for its hundreds of birds as well as its reptiles. Herons, pheasants and hawks can be seen. Bike racks and information on trails are available at the park headquarters, at the end of Carlin Street. (8)

Leaving the preserve, return to Sharrotts Road and turn RIGHT.

16.7 **Turn RIGHT at the end, onto Arthur Kill Road.**

Soon you will pass a couple of historic burial grounds on your left. St. Luke's Cemetery, opposite Zebra Place, and the Sleight family graveyard, just past Rossville Avenue, contain tombstones bearing the names of the area's earliest European settlers. You will recognize some of the names—Seguine, Poillon—from streets traveled on this tour. (9)

Continue STRAIGHT on Arthur Kill Road, underneath a highway overpass.

19.9 **Turn RIGHT at Arden Avenue, going uphill.**

20.7 **Turn LEFT at Woodrow Road, through a section of new housing development.**

The brand-new road is nice and smooth for easy cycling.

21.9 **Turn RIGHT at the end, onto Arthur Kill Road.**

22.5 **Bear LEFT at Drumgoole Road West.**

22.6 **Turn LEFT at the end, onto Richmond Avenue, which will lead you back to the Staten Island Mall.**

Bicycle Shops

The Bike Shop, 4026 Hylan Boulevard, Great Kills (718-948-5080)
Tottenville Hobby Center, 7515 Amboy Road, Tottenville (718-356-4220)

Guidebooks from The Countryman Press and Backcountry Publications

Written for people of all ages and experience, these popular and carefully prepared books feature detailed trail and tour directions, notes on points of interest and natural phenomena, maps and photographs.

Walks and Rambles Series
Walks and Rambles on the Delmarva Peninsula, $8.95
Walks and Rambles in Rhode Island, $8.95
Walks and Rambles in Westchester (NY) and Fairfield (CT) Counties, $7.95

Biking Series
25 Mountain Bike Tours in Vermont, $9.95
25 Bicycle Tours on Delmarva, $8.95
25 Bicycle Tours in Eastern Pennsylvania, $8.95
20 Bicycle Tours in the Finger Lakes, $7.95
25 Bicycle Tours in the Hudson Valley, $9.95
25 Bicycle Tours in Maine, $8.95
25 Bicycle Tours in New Hampshire, $7.95
25 Bicycle Tours in New Jersey, $8.95
20 Bicycle Tours in and around New York City, $7.95
25 Bicycle Tours in Vermont, $8.95

Canoeing Series
Canoe Camping Vermont and New Hampshire Rivers, $7.95
Canoeing Central New York, $10.95
Canoeing Massachusetts, Rhode Island and Connecticut, $7.95

Hiking Series
50 Hikes in the Adirondacks, $10.95
50 Hikes in Central New York, $9.95
50 Hikes in Central Pennsylvania, $9.95
50 Hikes in Connecticut, $10.95
50 Hikes in Eastern Pennsylvania, $10.95
50 Hikes in the Hudson Valley, $9.95
50 Hikes in Massachusetts, $10.95
50 More Hikes in New Hampshire, $9.95
50 Hikes in New Jersey, $10.95
50 Hikes in Northern Maine, $10.95
50 Hikes in Southern Maine, $10.95
50 Hikes in Vermont, $10.95
50 Hikes in West Virginia, $9.95
50 Hikes in Western Pennsylvania, $10.95
50 Hikes in the White Mountains, $10.95

Adirondack Series
Discover the Adirondack High Peaks $14.95
Discover the Central Adirondacks $8.95
Discover the Eastern Adirondacks $9.95
Discover the Northeastern Adirondacks $9.95
Discover the Northern Adirondacks $10.95
Discover the Northwestern Adirondacks $11.95
Discover the South Central Adirondacks $8.95
Discover the Southeastern Adirondacks $8.95
Discover the Southern Adirondacks $9.95
Discover the Southwestern Adirondacks $9.95
Discover the West Central Adirondacks $13.95

Ski-Touring Series
25 Ski Tours in Central New York $7.95
25 Ski Tours in New Hampshire $8.95

Other Guides
Maine: An Explorer's Guide $14.95
New England's Special Places $12.95
New York State's Special Places, $12.95
State Parks and Campgrounds in Northern New York $9.95
Vermont: An Explorer's Guide $14.95

The above titles are available at bookstores and at certain sporting goods stores or may be ordered directly from the publisher. For complete descriptions of these and other guides, write: The Countryman Press, P.O. Box 175, Woodstock, VT 05091.